# ST. IGNATIUS LOYOLA AND PRAYER

# ST. IGNATIUS LOYOLA AND PRAYER

## As seen in the Book of the Spiritual Exercises

*By*

### THE MOST REVEREND ALBAN GOODIER, S.J.

*Archbishop of Hierapolis*

## WITH A MEMOIR OF THE AUTHOR

*By*

### THE REVEREND H. KEANE, S.J.

NEW YORK, BOSTON, CINCINNATI, CHICAGO, SAN FRANCISCO

## BENZIGER BROTHERS

PRINTERS TO THE HOLY APOSTOLIC SEE

1940

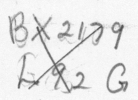
MADE AND PRINTED IN GREAT BRITAIN
FOR
BURNS OATES & WASHBOURNE LTD
PUBLISHERS TO THE HOLY SEE

# ARCHBISHOP GOODIER—A MEMOIR[1]

ALBAN GOODIER was born at Great Harwood, Lancashire, on April 14, 1869. He died with dramatic suddenness at Teignmouth on March 13, 1939, having all but completed his seventieth year. His life's story falls naturally into three periods : his career previous to his appointment to Bombay, his experiences in Bombay as Rector of St. Xavier's College and as Archbishop, and his life in London and at Teignmouth after his resignation of his see. On its outward side it is the story of the gradual development and unfolding under the influence of circumstances of a very simple, direct, and lovable character. From within it is the record of an ever-deepening and more clearly realised Catholic faith with increasing facility in its use for the help of others. Deeper and more intimate still lay the level of the development of his personal holiness, the secret of his power in the guidance of the perplexed or discouraged, and the impelling motive of his life.

At his death the Archbishop was not an old man, as age is reckoned to-day ; yet his life, especially in its last two periods, had been singularly full. He was not widely known outside a certain circle ;

[1] The substance of this Memoir has already appeared in *The Canadian Messenger of the Sacred Heart*, and is here reproduced by kind permission of the Editor.

but within it he counted for much. His reputation was made chiefly by his books, his retreats, and his preaching. His direct personal contacts were comparatively few ; but in the few, Catholic or non-Catholic, who were privileged to know him, especially in India, he evoked a measure of admiration and affection rare in an ecclesiastical dignitary. This fact alone would seem to indicate a personality out of the common. And he had an unusually happy combination of gifts of high range which he used with apparently effortless ease. Yet his intimates knew on what ungrudging labour much of this seeming facility was based. His writing, for instance, was very painstaking and subjected to repeated revision and correction before being given to the press. While to outward appearance he was a leisured man, in reality few worked harder than the Archbishop, even in the years when he might legitimately have claimed the right to less strenuous days. He gave generously of his time to others, taking a personal interest in their problems so long as he felt that he could be of help. But once convinced that an interviewer wished merely to discuss or argue and that the discussion would be in the main speculative, he began to feel his way towards ending the intercourse. For he was a busy man, with scant leisure for the discussion of speculative problems, however interesting in themselves. He had, too, his own deep convictions, based on Catholic faith, which he was never prepared to treat as mere opinions, liable to modification or revision as the outcome of discussion. It was part of his gift to be able to end such intercourse without a shadow of offence.

Interviewers were sometimes disappointed ; they were never hurt or annoyed.

Young Goodier entered Hodder, the Preparatory School for Stonyhurst, in January, 1881, moving up to the College in September, 1882. His school career was an indication of the gifts he was later to develop, especially on his literary side. His Latin and Greek prose secured him a high place in the class lists. He won the Senior English Essay prize, and as a boy began to write for the *Stonyhurst Magazine* essays or descriptive accounts of historic places he had visited. Besides a competent knowledge of the classics he carried away from Stonyhurst a love of English literature which he never lost, and a sensitiveness in the use of words which is so notable a feature in his own writing at its best. Stonyhurst also left a deep impression on his developing Faith. It could hardly be otherwise with one so sensitive to atmosphere. The apologetic value of such monuments of unbroken continuity as Old Hall, Ushaw, Downside, Stonyhurst, and other schools, inheritors of a recusant past, is considerable, and Goodier as a boy was, subconsciously perhaps, quick to recognise it. Once made, the recognition was later to emerge into full awareness. Thus in the volume published by Messrs. Cassell, entitled *Why I am and Why I am not a Catholic*, he can write :

' On the rolls of my school there were names which Shakespeare had glorified ; there were those amongst its professors whose very presence reminded the students of the price that had been paid to give them what they received. Among the treasures of the house were relics which told of a noble ancestry : vestments of Henry VII, caps and trinkets of Sir Thomas More, embroidery worked by Catherine of Aragon and her household, the Book of Hours of Mary Queen of Scots, the rope with which an English martyr had been bound, and the like ; and all these acquired, not by accident or purchase, as an antiquarian might acquire them, but by a proved inheritance that linked up the present with their first owners. There were portraits and manuscripts and books which declared by their mere existence, better than any syllogism, or any written chapter of history, that the line of the school was true, and unconsciously developed in the boy a love of the ancient faith, and a noble pride in England, which nothing in after life could undermine.

. . . Such was the education I received, not obtruded on me, scarcely ever mentioned ; while our classics and mathematics, our football and cricket, seemed to take up our energies, all the time we lived in an atmosphere redolent of the ancient Faith. We heard our Mass every morning as our forefathers had heard it ; we respected the statue of Our Lady as had been done of old at Winchester and Eton ; while others might look down on us as being out of the scheme of to-day, we could only be sorry for them because they had been despoiled of the one thing that mattered.'

One practical result of his boyhood at Stonyhurst was his desire for the religious life and his determination to ask for admission to the Jesuit noviceship, which he entered on September 7th, 1887. Seven years later he was back at Stonyhurst as a master and taught there for six years. In the

*Stonyhurst Magazine* for February, 1940, one who was under him during his last year of teaching is quoted as saying :

' I found Alban Goodier the best master I had at Stonyhurst. He really educated us. He always treated every boy with the greatest courtesy and reverence. He never " rated," and he never came down to a lower level in order to be a " big brother " to us. He was always kind, always patient, always the same. He taught the classics well, English better. He was fond of giving us general news and of telling us how to look at world affairs. No man did that better. I remember that the Boer War was being fought at the time, and on a dull morning in Lent when we were all weary and half-alive after morning studies, Goodier would begin schools after prayers by going to the blackboard and holding forth for forty minutes, maybe, before any other work, on the military situation in Africa. Then with his jerky little smile he would toss away his chalk, climb up into his desk and begin schools. I do not remember him punishing at all the whole year, and we never abused his leniency. He had all his experience behind him and we were lucky enough to have him in his best year. He read to us a great deal, mostly the poets, seldom stories, but he read well and we loved it all.'

Similar testimony to the Archbishop's gift for not merely teaching but educating is borne by Mr. J. M. N. Jeffries who wrote of him in the *Tablet*, March 18, 1939 :

' He taught us so that routine faded away and

the tiresome conning of facts vanished, though
we went on learning things and learning more
and more of them. . . . He brought the world
into our schoolroom.  We felt in some way that
we were doing something in a larger area than
we had ever known when we engaged on the
themes he set us, or listened to what he said,
or even when we ventured our young opinions
and he, in his turn, listened so marvellously
to us.

His very sensitiveness, which was so notable,
had an extraordinary influence upon us.  The
atmosphere of his class never became one of mere
discipline or indiscipline, the two phases which
had been familiar to us in previous schoolrooms.
The accustomed roles of master and boys, with
a social gulf between them, were not those which
he and we filled.  We found instead that this
grown and talented man seemed vitally affected
by our behaviour, by what we accomplished, or
what we failed to do.  This woke in us something
altogether new, a sense of our responsibility.  We
began to feel that we mattered in some way, and
were stung thereby to achievements and to a
level of conduct that (though we did not realise
it then) revolutionised the whole school.'

Such testimonies could be multiplied.  The fact
is that there was all through his life a strange
magnetism about Alban Goodier, which, for the
one it repelled, attracted ninety-nine others.  It
was based on a natural friendliness of disposition
and an innate sympathy, combined with a remarkable simplicity and directness of approach.  This

surely was the secret of his success with boys, whom he attracted not by athletic prowess nor by tales of thrilling adventure, but by sheer friendliness and naturalness. Perhaps he could himself hardly have explained his success or how it was achieved. He would have said that he was shy ; but his shyness drove him not to the extreme self-consciousness which is its ordinary result, but rather to a simple directness of approach, which at once put at their ease others no less shy, broke down reserves, and stimulated friendliness. Both the writers quoted note this characteristic. And it was so not only with boys but with all with whom he came into contact, whether then or later. It was the secret of his success with government officials, in the pulpit, in clergy retreats, and in chance intercourse with men of ideas and background totally different from his own. For a master it was an invaluable gift, evoking from boys a receptivity and readiness to learn which is one of the ideal conditions for successful teaching and for the intercourse of mind with mind.

In September, 1903, he was ordained at St. Beuno's, the Jesuit theological college in North Wales, since transferred to Heythrop in Oxfordshire. His first permanent appointment as a priest was in September, 1905, when he went to Manresa House, Roehampton. Here he taught Latin, Greek, and English in the Juniorate, or course of studies immediately following the novitiate. Three years later he was named Superior of the Juniors and Prefect of Studies, a post which he retained till he set sail for Bombay in the mid-October of 1914.

These nine years at Roehampton were very formative both intellectually and spiritually. He read widely both in the classics and in English prose and poetry, reading which he was able to turn to good account in his lectures. He began to be interested in the theory of education, especially in the Jesuit *Ratio Studiorum*, on which he published articles in the *Month*. About this time Messrs. Dent had begun the publication of the *Everyman Series*, and Goodier conceived the idea of a somewhat similar series of Catholic classics and of original work, which he inaugurated under the title of *The Catholic Library*, published by the Manresa Press. Some seventeen or eighteen volumes appeared ; but the venture was killed by the War and by his own transfer to Bombay.

On the spiritual side much of his development may be traced to the work he now began to do for religious communities. During these years he acted as chaplain to the Convent of the Sacred Heart at Roehampton. The work included weekly addresses to the children at the Sunday Mass. These soon began to attract attention by their freshness, directness, and simple earnestness ; and it took but little to establish him as a friend and adviser of any who were in difficulty or in search of guidance in spiritual matters. One of those who heard him writes of ' the intellectual bent which his sermons and lectures produced. St. Paul lived in one's mind ; his Epistles became alive, as did also the Psalms.' It was part of his gift as a preacher to make gospel scenes come to life. His vivid imagination ' saw the place,' as the Spiritual Exercises urge. But the setting, however vivid, was always subordinate to the personality of Christ, which was the central theme of all his addresses. Not all would at all times agree with his interpretation ; but all admitted its life and deep personal conviction. One who was present at his Sunday sermons to the children writes :

'Those who have read his printed works on the Life of Our Lord can realise what those weekly sermons were like. But to listen to him was an even greater inspiration than to read his written word. He had a voice and a way of speaking that immediately awakened interest and compelled attention. Fifteen minutes was the time he usually allowed himself to speak, having, as he would say, compassion on the children in his audience. But in those few minutes there were no wasted words. They provided matter for many hours of prayer.'

It was at this time that he first met Mother Janet Stuart, a kindred spirit to his own. His appreciation of her after her death might almost have been written of himself : 'Her very temperament exposed her to a larger share of suffering than falls to many people. The aspirations and cravings of her soul— the sense of distance and aloneness that enclosed her for years—the constant giving with no apparent return, these things would sometimes overwhelm her and often drove her into herself where none could follow, or out to the work of God where she might hide from herself' (*Life and Letters of J. E. Stuart*, p. 174). No friend of the Archbishop's but will recognise an autobiographical touch here, authentic if unconscious.

Of their meeting the writer just quoted adds :

'Their friendship began very characteristically
as the outcome of a meditation given to the children in retreat on "The Personality of Our
Lord." "Naturally from such a beginning," he
said, "we talked much of prayer and the value
of living with Our Lord during it, even if one did
no more." At that time, however, as he himself
told me, he was "reading everything he could
lay hands on about prayer—Alvarez de Paz, St.
Augustine, St. Bernard, St. Teresa, St. John of
the Cross, de Maumigny, Poulain, Juliana of
Norwich, St. Catherine of Siena (ever a favourite
saint of his), and many others," with the result,
as he said, that "I was *seeing* what before I had
only accepted, and finding that 'unless you
become as little children' referred even more to
the Kingdom of Prayer than to anything else.
Into the midst of these studies came Mother
Stuart. She got whatever I had to give her."
And it was with this abundance as a background
that he spoke in his weekly sermons. They were
never merely reproductions of the words and
thoughts of others, but all stamped with his own
marked personality.'[1]

This extensive reading in ascetics and hagio-
graphy was to bear fruit many years later in his
lectures at Heythrop on Ascetical and Mystical
Theology. In these he devotes a large section to
the study of Prayer, a subject of lifelong interest to
him alike in its theory and its practice. It was

[1] It was at this time and at the Sacred Heart Convent that
Goodier first met the future Cardinal Bourne, then Bishop of
Southwark. The acquaintance was later to ripen into an
intimate friendship.

during this period, too, that he began to give the Spiritual Exercises to various religious communities, especially to the convents of the Society of the Sacred Heart and of the Sisters of Notre Dame. His transparent sincerity, balanced judgement, and unfailing patience, together with his mastery of the Exercises, made him much sought after as a giver of retreats. His main effort was to help others to help themselves. One who had much experience of his retreats writes :

'If there was one rôle more than another which he refused to play it was that of spiritual " director." He positively objected to the phrase. He did not " direct." In all his spiritual relations with others his intention was to help souls to help themselves, to form their own judgements on their own acts. He listened with patience and sympathy to the perplexities and doubts that were placed before him ; he helped to unravel them. He explained first principles ; but he sought to make his penitents arrive by their own judgement at a just solution of their problems. They had to be absolutely sincere in their efforts to advance in the spiritual life, and he was quick to detect any lack of seriousness of purpose or any artificiality in those who sought help from him. He had a remarkable gift of discerning almost immediately the spiritual capacity of a soul. He suggested, encouraged, chided, but never forced the pace. Neither did he question his penitents ; on the contrary he respected the freedom of the soul, so that the confidences he received were given spontaneously and whole-heartedly.

B

His guidance in the matter of Prayer can be
summed up in his oft-repeated phrase : " Pray
as you can pray best." His patience with the
weak and fallen was inexhaustible. He had
the gift of understanding the long, as well as the
strong, pull of temptations, many of which he
had probably never experienced.'

His retreat work was an important part of his
life's achievement and was far-reaching in its influence. While there are many competent retreat-
givers it is granted to few really to excel in that
subtle combination of qualities which goes to make
the master, and Alban Goodier was one of the few.
His retreats were always based on the Spiritual
Exercises. Their form, their orderly development,
the heights to which they led were all thoroughly
Ignatian. But one of the secrets of the Exercises
(and there are many) lies in their indefinite adapt-
ability and pliability to the character and circumstances of the exercitant. Without such adaptation
they can easily become rigid and formal. Apart
from his personal holiness, the Archbishop's power
as a retreat-giver lay just here—his sympathy with
his audience, his quick appreciation of their needs,
and his gift of applying and developing the meditations of the Exercises along the lines of an understanding and personal message to themselves. He
used to say that he had only one retreat, which he
gave to the clergy, to religious, and to laymen.
That was true inasmuch as the background of his
retreats was always the same, the meditations of
the Exercises. But his method of treatment, his
illustrations, his applications were as varied as the

mentality of the audiences he was addressing. One thing alone was invariable, his intelligent sympathy and his entire devotion during the retreat to their spiritual interests and needs. There was also the contact of mind with mind, of an intelligence that was cultured, refined, experienced, and with no trace of narrowness ; and above all of heart with heart. The generosity of his own disposition was an inspiration to the self-centred and egotistic, and still more to the wounded or bruised soul for which the shocks of life had been wellnigh too severe. If we now add to this his own radiant holiness, his deep appreciation of spiritual things, his almost Pauline love of Christ, which for all its attractiveness abated no jot of the gospel of pain and suffering, we have the key to the undoubted success of his retreats.

With all this, too, he was detached. There was a certain elusiveness about him, a supernatural aloofness, which added to his power. For he was a true ascetic, but with an asceticism which attracted rather than repelled. One felt that he lived with God, yet so as to energise rather than atrophy his natural human qualities of sympathy and affectionateness, much as one feels it in Teresa of Avila or John of the Cross. There were times when he felt poignantly and when his sense of frustration, whether in his own work or that of the Church, seemed to fill his horizon. But these were but passing moods revealed only to his intimates. Habitually he lived in that serenity of outlook, that trust in God, and that confidence in the ultimate triumph of truth which he displays so masterfully in his book, *The Inner Life of the Catholic.*

This retreat work was not merely helpful to others. It was also moulding his own interior life. Under its influence his mind began more and more to take its colour and direction from the Spiritual Exercises. His later writings show this in their very titles : *Christ the Model of Manhood*, *The Passion and Death of Our Lord*, *The Risen Jesus*, *The Life that was Light*, *The Public Life of Our Lord*. All alike are Christocentric and reflect the spiritual ideals of the disciple of St. Ignatius of Loyola. The Christ of whom he wrote was not the Christ of historical study and research, but, as he himself avers in his preface to *The Public Life*, the living Christ of yesterday, to-day, and forever. The whole effect of his writing and teaching was to make this Christ real for the men and women of his time.

He had now spent nine years at Roehampton, and they were among the happiest of his life. His relations with his Juniors were uniformly pleasant. He was at the height of his powers as a teacher, and the work interested him absorbingly. The vacations furnished an even deeper interest, his retreat work, exhausting but stimulating. It made him conscious of his gift for helping others. It clarified and deepened his thoughts on many spiritual subjects. It brought him into contact with widely different types, especially with generous souls living heroically lives that were to outward view humdrum and prosaic. It threw his thoughts back more and more on to the secret workings of grace, the indwelling of the Holy Spirit and His action in the heart of the individual. It opened vistas of closer intimacy with God. Meanwhile he was gaining a deeper insight into the profundities of the Spiritual Exercises, so easily missed by the casual reader and even by the casual retreat-giver.

Yet it might be said with truth that thus far his life had been comparatively sheltered and narrow. He had to his account an exceptionally successful record as a teacher, a character rich in potentiality, a subtle and far-reaching influence on others, a literary gift as yet somewhat undeveloped, or at least not fully exercised, in addition to the fund of spiritual discernment that went with his priesthood and religious profession. But with all these positive assets he was still untried. He had scaled no heights, nor even matched himself against others. He was now to be tested in circumstances which were to him of no ordinary difficulty, and he was to emerge from the ordeal spiritually and intellectually strengthened and broadened for the work he had yet to do. It was to cost, as all such testings must. But if he was to lose his life, he was also to find it. In the autumn of 1914 came the call to the East.

St. Xavier's university college, Bombay, was in charge of the German Jesuit Fathers who had taken over the Bombay-Poona Mission in 1858. Their record of public service was high and it was therefore not without much hesitation and reluctance that shortly after the outbreak of the war in August, 1914, the question of their internment was decided upon. Even then the Government was unwilling to cripple the college and asked for the internment only of as many as could be spared, leaving a skeleton staff to carry on the work of the university until such time as substitutes could be found. The Superior at once applied to the English Jesuit

Provincial, Father John Wright, to send a capable priest as Principal of the college and Director of Studies. The Provincial selected Father Goodier for the post.

In many ways the choice was ideal. The new Principal had been all his life engaged in education. He was now forty-five ; his judgement was well balanced, his health good, and his mind had reached its maturity without losing any of its youthful suppleness. He accepted the appointment willingly, even eagerly, and by mid-October he had sailed for Bombay. He arrived in early November and his influence began at once to be felt. From the beginning he acted as intermediary between the German Fathers and the Government and was soon able to secure valuable concessions on the difficult question of internment. On the academic side his success was assured from the outset. He brought to his work a vigour of mind and a sympathetic knowledge of English literature, the subject in which he lectured, which made an immediate impression. In a very short time he had made valuable acquaintances in university circles, among the diverse Indian people of Bombay, and with Government officials. The result was a welcome increase in prestige for the Catholic community in the city. In his appreciation of the Archbishop in the *Catholic Herald*, March 24th, 1939, Father Ernest Hull wrote of this time :

' His mind was surprisingly fertile and practical in schemes and enterprises, and he had a knack of arousing enthusiasm in those who could help to carry them out. He threw himself into founding debating clubs and academies at the College, and had them in full running while anyone else would have been puzzling how to begin.'

And in a private letter he added : ' He did very well in his work in the College and with the Government and became intimate with the Governor. The College at this time had 1200 students.'

About June, 1915, total internment of the German staff was decided upon and the order was to be carried out as soon as possible. As Principal, Father Goodier took advantage of the vacation to return to England in search of masters of university standing. He secured three, returning with them in November. On his arrival he was appointed Rector of St. Xavier's. He was also made a Fellow and Syndic of the University and a Justice of the Peace. A layman who was with him at this time writes :

' The position was one calling for the greatest tact as well as knowledge. Father Goodier by his scholarly learning, personality, holiness, and charm won all hearts. The German Fathers respected him, the Indians admired him and were inspired by him, and the European community felt they had a friend. . . . Father Goodier in those difficult days so won the confidence of the Governor that (I know it for a fact) he would not deport or intern clergy of foreign extraction belonging to an enemy nation without Father Goodier's consent or knowledge. It was a great trust and involved a great personal responsibility ; but he stood the test and was trusted by both sides.'

In September, 1916, the Ordinary of Bombay, Archbishop Jurgens, died and for some time the see remained vacant. Owing to war conditions the choice of a successor was a perplexing one. After much deliberation the name of Alban Goodier was put at the head of the terna sent to Rome. He was accepted by the Holy See and consecrated by Cardinal Bourne at Westminster Cathedral on December 22, 1919. On January 5, 1920, he sailed for Bombay, arriving there on January 27.

Of the success of the new Archbishop's pastoral work there can be no doubt. He left his mark on the spiritual, moral, and social life of Bombay and its environs. St. Catherine's Rescue Home at Andheri, St. Anthony's Home for the Destitute, St. Elizabeth's Nursing Home are his monuments. He found an outlet for a long imprisoned zeal which could now spend itself freely in the service of the sick and unfortunate. Such work was to him sheer joy. From the beginning he was in close contact with the Good Shepherd nuns with whose selfless work he had a profound sympathy. To quote Father Hull once more :

' There was one rapid series of developments : hospitals, hostels for girls and for young men, convent schools, parish schools, all of which flourished and proved permanent. He hardly had to appeal for money, of which much was needed. It flowed out as from a reservoir. " Dr. Goodier's Charities " was the title of the fund, which grew into a household word. He became at once " the idol of the people." '

A difficulty commonly felt by English Catholic residents in an Indian city is lack of contact with the clergy. Since Catholic India is apportioned between missionaries of so many European nations it is comparatively rare to find priests of English extraction or with knowledge of English conditions and mentality. To meet this difficulty the Archbishop inaugurated a ' European Catholic Union ' with a view to fostering a common European Catholic social life and charitable effort. With a somewhat similar object he also formed a ' Catholic Charities Organisation ' to prevent overlapping of charitable work and to secure a due apportioning of Catholic charitable funds. In the same connection he invigorated and breathed new life into the St. Vincent de Paul Society. Thenceforth all Catholic social and charitable activity in Bombay centred in the Archbishop, and his work met with instant recognition on the part of Catholics and non-Catholics alike.

But with all this brilliance of achievement there went a shadow, so deep at times as almost to seem like an eclipse. The trouble was the double jurisdiction. The situation with which the Archbishop was faced was the outcome of a highly complicated historical development which had its roots in the Portuguese missionary expansion of the sixteenth century and the subsequent missionary enterprise of Propaganda in the seventeenth century. Within the territory of Bombay certain churches and congregations were subject, not to the Archbishop of Bombay but to the Bishop of Damaun, Portuguese territory to the north of Bombay and a suffragan diocese of the Metropolitan See ruled over by the

Patriarch of Goa. In practice it meant that there were at this time in Bombay two ecclesiastical authorities, the British Archbishop of Bombay, appointed through Propaganda, and the Portuguese Bishop of Damaun, appointed through the Patronage (*padroado*) which had been conferred by the Popes on the Crown of Portugal. This meant overlapping, confusion, division of loyalties, friction. Given the situation, such things were inevitable and could not be controlled. Archbishop Goodier was above all else a peaceable soul. The whole bent of his mind and disposition was towards concord, harmony, the sense of united effort. He could well understand and allow for differences of opinion, diversities based on divergent points of view. He was far from wishing everyone to be like-minded with himself. But it was repugnant to him in the extreme to have to fight for what he felt was but his normal due, most of all to have to fight against another ecclesiastical authority. Not that there was personal conflict between the Archbishop and the Patriarch. There was not. It was rather a conflict of interests, of loyalties. However single-minded and pure-intentioned the two principals, they could not control the mentality of their subjects, least of all when the controversy was conducted on lines of nationalism and national privileges, to the undoubted and understandable scandal of the non-Catholic onlooker. One has only to recall the almost hypersensitive temperament of Archbishop Goodier, his high idealism, his loathing for intrigue or clever trickery, utterly alien from his whole habit of mind, to realise in what a Nessus-robe of irritation and annoyance he now found himself enveloped. The distress was unceasing, intolerable, at times almost maddening. As Father Hull well says :

' To a prelate, of dry, matter-of-fact temperament, who could calmly acquiesce in " making the best of a bad job," the situation was tolerable : but to Archbishop Goodier, with his high idealism, his acute susceptibility, his shrinking from conflict and dread of estrangement—and above all his inability to play a game of move and counter-move and enjoy it as a sport—the situation was desperate, unbearable, and soon grew into a nightmare. It told on his health, his nerve, his temper. He alternated pitifully between the deepest grief and the highest indignation.'

The strain, both mental and physical, was severe. Every element in the complex conflict was entirely new and unfamiliar. Decisions were difficult to take and always attended with risk. It was intolerable, he felt, to do nothing, to pass over in silence actions which cried aloud for protest, yet in which remonstrance might do more harm than good. But what could one do, and what would be the result? Small wonder that, as he had written of Mother Stuart, ' these things would sometimes overwhelm him and often drove him into himself where none could follow.'

As the months passed his health, hitherto uniformly good, though never robust, began to show signs of the nervous strain to which it was daily exposed. For the first time in his experience he suffered from sudden and unexpected fainting

fits, often mercifully concealed from others. These
at the time he lightly dismissed as slight heart-
attacks, though, had he but known it, they were
a symptom and a warning. The work of government, always uncongenial, began gradually to
weigh more heavily upon him. For five years he
endured ; but it became increasingly clear that the
situation could not be effectively handled without
conflict to a decision, and for conflict he felt no
least inclination. Fortunately he was due for his
*Ad limina* visit to Rome in 1925. He resolved to
make it as soon as possible. He would then lay
the whole matter before Propaganda and press for
a solution, even if it meant tendering his own
resignation. To his friends he was emphatic that
the present state of affairs must be mended or
ended. He himself was in favour of ending it by
the appointment of a single Ordinary in Bombay,
alternately a British and a Portuguese subject, free
from the complication of a second jurisdiction.

Accordingly, in the early days of January, 1925,
he sailed for Rome. He was received alike by the
Holy Father and the Congregation of Propaganda
with every mark of appreciation and sympathy.
Propaganda was fully alive, he found, to the perplexities of a situation which was none of its making.
It asked him for a full report on the difficulties
experienced in practical working and for any suggestions he might have by way of solution or miti-
gation. It noted his offer of resignation as a help
towards a solution, but declined to express any
opinion until it had had time for a complete and
deliberate review of the situation. The Archbishop
then spent some weeks in Rome drafting his report.

After a visit to England he returned to Rome and from there went to Palestine, where he spent two months. In the early days of November he was back again in London.

In England, little though he suspected it, he was to begin fourteen years of diversified but most fruitful work. He arrived tired, depressed, uncertain of his future, half repentant of the offer to resign, and full of affectionate regrets for the work he had left in India. Though nothing was yet settled, he was haunted by a presentiment that he would never go back to Bombay. After a few visits to friends in Lancashire, Oxford, and elsewhere he returned to London with no very definite plans, awaiting the decision of Propaganda. He called on Cardinal Bourne, who welcomed him with outstretched arms. His kindness met with an immediate response from the Archbishop, who offered himself to help in any way he could, so long as he remained in England, in the immense work which devolves on the Ordinary of Westminster. The Cardinal, who was beginning to feel his years, readily accepted the offer. This was the beginning of a close intimacy which was one of the Archbishop's greatest consolations and which survived unimpaired until the Cardinal's death.

In the months that followed the Archbishop was able to relieve the Cardinal in many ways, taking his place at meetings and on committees, confirming, ordaining, and preaching. Once more his simplicity and directness triumphed, and his welcome was everywhere assured.

It was not till September of the following year, 1926, that any very definite news reached him

from Rome. Propaganda accepted his offer of
resignation which he now formally tendered on
September 8. This meant that he was not to return
to Bombay. Though he had long expected it, the
blow was severe. During this trying time Cardinal
Bourne was a tower of strength and gave him
many proofs of his personal friendship. He had
a standing invitation to Archbishop's House where
a room was always at his disposal, and the Cardinal
made no secret of his high esteem for his advice
and help. In October he was transferred to the
titular see of Hierapolis in Phrygia. Ultimately,
in May, 1928, the Holy See signed a Concordat
with the Portuguese Government by which the
jurisdiction of the Patriarch of Goa was restricted
to Portuguese territory, and an agreement reached
by which the Archbishop of Bombay should be
alternately of British and Portuguese nationality.
This was the very solution of the difficulty which
Archbishop Goodier had himself proposed.

The Cardinal pressed him to stay on in the
archdiocese. There was plenty of work of the kind
that he would do admirably, and he might do as
much or as little as he wished. He delicately conveyed to him also how gratified he would be to
have him, if not as formal Coadjutor (though he
was to take that charge for a short time later), at
least as a helper on whom he might rely. No
request could have been more opportune. It came
from a friend and was proffered with a delicacy
which made it difficult to reject. To the Archbishop it was a present help in time of trouble.
With his resignation accepted and now an accomplished fact, the uncertainty of the future had

begun to weigh on his mind. As a religious he
was not likely to receive a territorial episcopal
appointment, and without episcopal duties there
was no prospect save that of a return, with no
very definite line of work, to a religious house.

No man was more loyal than Alban Goodier,
none more ready to undertake with his whole heart
any task his Superiors might assign him. Accordingly, before accepting the Cardinal's offer he put
himself unreservedly at the disposal of the Jesuit
Provincial for any work he might wish him to do.
The latter, however, knowing the Cardinal's need
and the excellence of the service the Archbishop
could give, urged him to accept the proposal, only
asking that he would be willing to undertake occa-
sional community retreats. The result was that
he accepted the offer, and for the next two years
was engaged in a great variety of work in the archdiocese. This included much preaching up and
down the London area, addresses and conferences
of all sorts, clergy retreats, as well as the superin-
tendence for some time of the House for Late
Vocations at Edmonton. He soon became more
widely known and the calls on his time began to
multiply. London, however, did not suit his
health. He suffered from insomnia and from a
gradually increasing debility which, though it did
not seriously interfere with his work, took its toll
on his reserves of strength. In the February of
1928 an opportunity of escape providentially
occurred. The chaplain of the Benedictine nuns
at Teignmouth was compelled by ill-health to ask
for long leave of absence, and the Archbishop was
invited to take his place for the time being. Thus

began his connection with Teignmouth which was never severed till his death. The position was ideal. The place was restful and quiet. It was removed from London, yet not too far. He was free from telephones and callers. His time was his own and the convent surroundings were thoroughly congenial. He proposed the matter to the Cardinal as a mere temporary respite, as at first it promised to be. The Cardinal, who knew something of the cost at which he had given such generous and effective help for the past two years, readily agreed to his taking the appointment. Before the end of February the Archbishop was installed at the convent as temporary chaplain.

The chaplain's duties were not onerous and there were welcome intervals of leisure. These he devoted for the most part to writing. Within a few years he wrote *Jesus Christ Model of Manhood*, *About the Old Testament*, *The Bible for Every Day*, *The Inner Life of the Catholic*, *The Life that was Light*, *Saints for Sinners*, *The Passion and Death of Our Lord*, and what he always regarded as his chief work, *The Public Life of Our Lord*. The list is by no means exhaustive, as a glance at Messrs. Burns, Oates and Washbourne's catalogue will show. In addition to this he reviewed regularly for the *Month*, to which, as well as to other periodicals, he frequently contributed. The temporary chaplaincy proved longer than he had anticipated, and it was not till August, 1930, that, on the return of the regular chaplain, he went back to London at the Cardinal's special request.

The fact was that the latter really missed the Archbishop's help and took the first opportunity of securing him once more for the archdiocese. He now proposed to make him his Coadjutor, and, that he might have a residence of his own, to name him parish priest of St. Mary's, Cadogan Gardens, Chelsea. The Archbishop readily accepted the joint office, though not without misgiving as to the compatibility of the two charges, a misgiving which the event was to justify. No doubt there are men who could have combined both offices quite successfully ; but to a meticulously conscientious temperament such as the Archbishop's the work of a parish priest was an absorbing task which left little leisure for other activities. Moreover, it put him back once more into the atmosphere of callers and telephones, and interviewers which he had already found so distressing. However, he threw himself wholeheartedly into the work, his efforts warmly seconded by the two priests who had been assigned as his assistants, on whom he entirely relied for the details of parish routine, and who on their side found in him an ideal Chief. Of the effect of his work one who saw much of him and it at the time writes :

' When he went to St. Mary's his first expressed wish was for an oratory where he could retire for meditation and prayer, and he spent a considerable time in what it was found possible to arrange for him in an alcove between the sacristy and the chancel.

He was wont to say the seven o'clock Mass daily, and he usually preached at the Sunday evening service, the congregation at which soon rose from an average of twenty to a number that

exceeded the seating capacity of the church.
Yet these Sunday evening sermons were most
simple little Gospel expositions, but at the same
time seemed to be searching as well as convincing
and to leave the impression of listening to one
who was not only a teacher but also, one felt, a
sympathiser and a friend.'

Parochial work in a busy parish leaves little
leisure for other occupations, least of all for anything like serious writing. With it was combined
the special work he had to do for the Cardinal,
which meant frequent absences from home, functions, social gatherings and the like, all of which,
however excellent in themselves, make great demands on nervous energy. The Archbishop was
a deeply conscientious parish priest. He was at
pains to be accessible to all. He more than once
protested when people thought that ' he must not
be disturbed.' The result was often a stream of
parochial callers, to whom he never denied himself
and which effectively put an end to any settling
down to literary work.

Meanwhile other work was multiplying. Towards
the end of 1930 the Secretary of State for the
Colonies formed an Advisory Committee to debate
questions connected with Colonial Religious Education. Its members consisted of representatives of
the various religious bodies, and at the Cardinal's
request Archbishop Goodier represented the Catholic Church. The Committee met once a month
under the chairmanship of Lord Lurgan. Various
sub-committees dealt with detailed matters of
routine, while *ad hoc* committees were appointed

with special terms of reference.  Of one of these
the Archbishop was Chairman.  In conjunction
with the late Mgr. Basil Gudgeon of the A.P.F. he
drew up a Syllabus of Instruction for intending
missionaries, which was favourably received by the
Advisory Committee and put into the syllabuses
of the two Training Colleges at Strawberry Hill,
Twickenham, and St. Charles's Square, North
Kensington, for men and women respectively.
Father A. E. Howell, Superior in England of the
White Fathers, was also a member of this sub-
committee and recalls the deep conscientiousness
and sincerity of the Archbishop's work and his
excellent chairmanship.  During all this period he
was in close touch with Archbishop, now Cardinal,
Hinsley, who was then Apostolic Delegate in Africa
and in immediate contact with native educational
problems.

In November, 1931, he was beginning seriously
to feel the strain of the combined offices of Coadjutor
and parish priest, and he once more retired to
Teignmouth, this time as a guest.  The warmth
of his welcome suggested the idea that, if only he
could free himself from his London engagements,
the convent would be an ideal place in which to
work.  He could live there and go up to London
as his appointments required.  Twelve months
later the idea was carried out and he made Teignmouth his permanent home till his death.  The
Cardinal generously consented to release him from
his double office on condition that he kept in touch
with Westminster and that he might have the
benefit of his services in any special urgency.  The
condition was easily satisfied, as he had to visit

London once a month for the Colonial Office
meetings, when he made a point of calling on the
Cardinal and learning his wishes as to any special
work in prospect.

For another seven years he was to live continu-
ously at the convent in Teignmouth. By this
time he had become well known in England as a
writer, preacher, and retreat-giver. His *Public
Life of Our Lord*, which he had written during his
previous stay at the convent as chaplain and
published in 1930, had met with a very favourable
reception and been several times reprinted. His
retreat work grew enormously. He was frequently
engaged two years ahead and had to refuse almost
as many applications as he accepted. He always
gave preference to clergy retreats or retreats to
religious men. In regard to convents, he refused
all applications from institutes to whose communities he had not given retreats before these days at
Teignmouth.

As a preacher for special occasions—a work for
which he was now much in demand—he was singularly effective. His manner was simple in the
extreme, yet impressive from its very simplicity. He
always spoke as one having a message for his
hearers, the full import of which he could not
then convey. There was more to be said than
the time at his disposal or the nature of the occasion would perhaps allow. From the first he could
attract and hold an audience, and dismiss them
thoughtful and eager to hear him again. He
spoke, too, as one with a deep experience of men
and their ways, their weakness and their greatness
—more often perhaps of their greatness—and of

heroic lives lived under trying conditions. His language was measured, as though he had weighed every word, and was never denunciatory. He encouraged and stirred hope, even when he lamented that many knew so little of the things that were to their peace. Back of it all was an intense earnestness and a deep and infectious conviction that Christ and His teaching were the sole solution of the individual's as of the world's troubles. Even here he never hectored or declaimed ; but he unfailingly conveyed the depth of his own conviction and the fervour with which he held it. On more important occasions he wrote his sermons *in extenso*. Sometimes he read them, and he read well. But he never preached without careful preparation, without a good deal of note-taking and of arrangement and rearrangement of matter. The spontaneity and naturalness of so much that he said in public was due just to this careful preparatory thought.

What he always regarded as his chief written work was his *The Public Life of Our Lord Jesus Christ* published, as has been said, in two volumes by Burns Oates & Washbourne in 1930. In the Introduction he tells us that : ' Often in the last forty years the author has planned its scope ; still more often he has written separate chapters and then has thrown them away ; only after a visit to the Holy Land in 1925 did the whole picture seem to come together, and to stand out as a consistent whole before him in a way that encouraged him to face the task he had often before wished to undertake.' He next relates how he wrote a first version, which he left untouched for a year. He

then entirely re-wrote it, ' and while much was
eliminated, much more was added and expanded.'
' Throughout the years during which the two ver-
sions were written he had constantly before himself
the question : What was Our Lord, as a man,
like ?   What is He like to-day ? '

On the title-page he describes his work as ' An
Interpretation,' and the description is accurate.   It
has been said with truth that no definitive Life of
Our Lord can ever be written.   All ' Lives ' are
but interpretations of a personality which defies
human analysis.   As such they must be to some
degree subjective and reflect the mentality of the
writer.   The Archbishop's work is no exception.
But it reflects a mind peculiarly qualified to grapple
with the question proposed by himself as his term
of reference : What was Our Lord, as a Man,
like ?   Not only was he intimately familiar with
every line of the four gospels, but he had read
widely in Catholic and non-Catholic gospel studies ;
he had seen the gospel at work in all sorts of men
and women in both East and West, and he had
behind him forty years of prayerful pondering and
meditation on its lessons.   His acquaintance with
Palestine and his knowledge of the East give a
personal touch to his descriptions besides furnishing
him with many a vivid pen-picture of the Galilean
lake and hills and villages.   His pastoral journeys
in India had familiarised him with Oriental peasant
life, its poverty and squalor, and its stoic endurance
of disease and death.   A leper was to him no con-
jectural figure; he had seen and talked and sympa-
thised with the stricken victims of the disease.

He was thus in many ways qualified to visualise

the *mise-en-scène* of the gospel story, and he used with telling effect his powers of simple description. Of the success of the book there can be no doubt. It sold well both in England and America and the reviewers were loud in its praise. Some critics, however, thought they detected a certain lack of virility in the portrayal, a tendency to overstress the emotional, pathetic side, to insist overmuch on the failure of Christ rather than on His triumph. Too frequently, they felt, He was represented as ' hurt,' ' wounded,' ' insulted,' and even as acting under the influence of these emotions, whereas the evangelists in their objective narrative seldom stress such feelings. But it is just here, surely, that interpretation begins, and it must be coloured by the mentality of the interpreter. It is tempting to contrast the book with Père Lagrange's masterly *Évangile de Jésus-Christ*,[1] a more comprehensive work of surer touch and firmer texture. But the comparison is perhaps hardly fair. Père Lagrange was a biblical scholar of the first rank and of immense erudition, which in the work in question he combines with a piety as devotional as it is childlike and unobtrusive. The two books differ considerably in scope, the Archbishop explicitly limiting himself to an interpretation of the human side of Our Lord as seen in His Public Life. Nor would he for a moment have dreamed of comparison with so high an authority as Père Lagrange.

These criticisms apart, the book is a great one of its kind. It brought Jesus of Nazareth before its thousands of readers in vivid, telling, simple language. It made the gospel story ' come to life,'

[1] An excellent English translation is published by Burns Oates and Washbourne.

as used to be said of its author's preaching in his early days at Roehampton. He was more than satisfied by the generally favourable reception with which it met, and which evoked an almost immediate increase in the number of applications for retreats which he received.

It was characteristic of the Archbishop to lend his aid generously to any cause which sought to promote the good of religion. Hence, when in 1935 the Prior of the Canons Regular at Bodmin, Very Rev. R. A. McElroy, C.R.L., proposed a Catholic Summer School to discuss the history of Catholicity in Devon and Cornwall, he felt that he could rely on the Archbishop's support, which was readily given. The first meeting was held at Truro in July 1935. It was well attended and aroused much enthusiasm. The Archbishop lectured on *Pelagius the Briton*, and, *Pelagius and Pelagianism*, seeking to establish a connection between Pelagius and the British Church in the West, and to account for his errors as an over-vehement and unbalanced protest against a false Oriental mysticism.[1] The School closed on August 2 with High Mass at the Priory church, Bodmin. The Archbishop preached appealing vividly to the Catholic life of British and pre-Reformation Cornwall and Devon, and emphasising the importance of the congress as an undeniable omen of present vitality and future development.

Next year the School was duplicated at Truro and Bodmin. The Archbishop lectured on St. Thomas More and again preached the closing

[1] Both lectures are reproduced in the volume, *History and Religion*, B.O.W., 1937.

sermon on the subject of St. Augustine, Apostle of England. In 1937 the attendance showed some falling off in numbers, and in 1938 it was thought wiser, owing to the disturbed state of Europe, not to attempt it. But it was a brave venture, and it is hoped that it may yet be revived. Recalling the Archbishop's association with the work the Prior wrote :

' He gave me the greatest encouragement, and, what was more, by his presence and participation lifted the effort to a higher level than it could possibly have attained without him. Had he withheld encouragement, I might have felt too faint-hearted to do anything.'

During the last five or six years of his life he lectured on Ascetical Theology at the Jesuit theological college at Heythrop. His lectures were both historical and dogmatic, covering the whole field from the apostolic age down to our own day. All who heard them are agreed that they were models of concise exposition combined with lucidity and depth. He received the compliment, unique surely for a theological lecturer, of a request from those who had followed the course to be allowed to attend it a second time. The lectures have since been published by Burns, Oates, and Washbourne under the title, *An Introduction to Ascetical and Mystical Theology*. They are an illuminating document on the interior life of the Archbishop.

His teaching on prayer had already been concisely stated in two sentences in the preface to *The Life that was Light* : ' Prayer is one's own realisation of God and the supernatural, not the mere analysis of spiritual things.' And again :

' Prayer is thought raised to vision : it is abstrac-
tion turned to reality.' The ideas thus briefly
formulated are developed at length in the *Introduction*, pp. 130–209.

He starts with the fundamental principle that
prayer is not an end in itself, but a means to perfection, that is, to the love of God. He insists much on
the value of vocal prayer, the ordinary prayer of
night and morning for instance, provided that such
prayers are said seriously and not as mere matters of
routine. Thus :

' First, there are the actual prayers which every
believing Christian takes as part of his ordinary
life. He accepts them as the bonds which bind
him every day to the supernatural, even though
the rest of his day is very natural and mundane
indeed. . . . They remind him, and he wishes
to be reminded, that behind the life which he
lives, of eating and drinking, of work and
pleasure, of success and failure, there is another
which he also lives, and which will continue
when the present excitement is over. They are
the prayers which may be appointed for us, like
the Breviary of the priest, or those arranged and
settled for ourselves, like the morning and evening
oblation. They come and go with each day,
there is something monotonous, even mechanical,
about them ; but it is important to remember that
they are, even in their monotony, a distant means
to the making of the perfect man. The soul that
aspires to any degree of perfection will try never
to omit them ; below its fixed regime of prayer
it will try never to allow itself to go ' (pp. 131–2).

Such prayer, faithfully persevered in, will inevitably lead to the desire for more and thus gradually to living the life of prayer, the 'praying without ceasing' of St. Paul. 'By this is meant the attitude of prayer in all one's life, so that life itself is prayer; the raising of the mind and heart to God in every action of every day' (p. 133). This he analyses into 'conscious,' 'when definitely we speak to God in the midst of our ordinary daily actions'; 'subconscious,' 'when the soul is trained, and becomes accustomed, to fall back on God at vacant intervals'; and 'unconscious,' 'meaning that kind of spiritual instinct which the soul of prayer, or of prayerfulness, unconsciously develops, enabling it to "judge all things" in the light and sight of God' (p. 134).

He next treats of the three 'Ways,' purgative, illuminative, and unitive, and of the prayer proper to each. He rightly insists that for the majority of souls the three ways intertwine. 'Indeed sometimes a soul may be in two "ways" at once, or even in all three, in the sense that it may have some experience of them all at much the same time' (p. 142). With St. Teresa and St. John of the Cross he is emphatic that in the spiritual life the Purgative Way can never be wholly discarded, and that before any other state can be reached, it must have become more or less permanent. Sorrow for past sin and, in general, a horror of sin, is the foundation of all genuine spiritual life. Hence the prayer of the Purgative Way will seek forgiveness and purification, the desire 'to be wholly such that His love may be happy in the sight of me.' The realisation of God and the supernatural, of oneself and one's

shame and guilt, petition for help, for healing, for
courage and strength not to relapse, such are the
chief features of the prayer of the Purgative Way
(pp. 142–7).

' I am the light of the world.  He that followeth
me walketh not in darkness, but shall have the
light of life '—such is the Light of the Illuminative
Way, and its prayer is naturally to know, love, and
follow Christ more closely.  ' The soul has its
eyes turned, henceforth, on a Person far more
attractive, and far more worth contemplating, than
its miserable little self.  It realises itself less and
God and Jesus more, studies itself less and them
more, cares for itself less and them more ; in the end
puts off self altogether and puts on Jesus Christ,
judging itself and all things in His light alone '
(p. 165).  Hence it advances to the prayer of love
and to affective prayer, or the prayer of greater
realisation as the Archbishop prefers to call it.
(He maintains that all prayer worthy of the name
is affective.)  He quotes St. Teresa to the effect that
in practice the highest kind of prayer for any soul
is that which best suits it at any given stage of its
growth.  Hence the value of preparation before and
reflection after sustained prayer, meditation, or
contemplation.  Else affective prayer is liable to
come to a standstill (pp. 167–8).  Avoiding the
Bérullian-Ignatian controversy, so stressed by H.
Bremond, he states simply that Illuminative Prayer
is occupied primarily with the Person of Christ and
with the mysteries and events of His life, quoting
in his support St. Teresa, St. Peter of Alcantara,
and Louis of Granada.  Its effect will be to make
Our Lord more of a reality, to live with Him, hence

to ' see things as God sees them, to feel about
things as God feels about them ' and to judge of
life accordingly. The result will be a greater
simplification of the whole of the spiritual life, no
longer two lives but one, of prayer and action, the
combination of active and contemplative, the
absorption of the natural by the supernatural. The
soul thus learns to ' pray always.' It ' lives, now not
it, but Christ lives in it ' (pp. 169–70). There
follows a chapter on the dangers of Illuminative
Prayer—sentimentality, self-complacency, the reac-
tion to dryness—together with a most important
chapter on mortification and the practice of the
virtues. The Archbishop is at one with all the
great teachers of the spiritual life in his insistence
that there is no true prayer without mortification.
In this he but echoes St. Teresa's ' Prayer and self-
indulgence go ill together.'

The rest of the book, pp. 186–209, is occupied
with the Unitive Way and the Prayer of Contemplation. Here we cannot do better than send the
reader to the book itself. He will find in the
Archbishop's treatment a lucidity which is evidence
of a wide course of reading, combined with the
results of personal experience alike in the use of
unitive prayer and in the guidance of those gifted
with it. Throughout he avoids barren controversy
and is content to rely as his main authorities on St.
Teresa and St. John of the Cross, than whom there
are no greater in the Church's teaching on the
Mystical Life. He distinguishes clearly between
acquired and infused contemplation, insisting with
St. Teresa that the latter is a sheer gift of God, to the
acquiring of which no efforts of ours can contribute

anything. As to the former, ' in principle at least
the Way of Union is open to all.' And again,
' For all . . . who truly and effectually seek
spiritual perfection as the first object of their lives,
the Unitive Way should be, not only possible, not
only lawful, but a natural conclusion to the progress
they have made ' (p. 188). He encourages desire
of this Way, only warning us with St. Teresa that
to strain after it is the surest way to lose it. His
practical conclusion he states as follows :

> ' In practice, then, whatever one may ambition
> or wish for, the soul that would go as far as God
> will draw it to go should take itself as it finds
> itself at any given stage, praying and striving
> for perfection as it can there and then ; never
> straining too much after what may be beyond
> its reach, for that can only lead to self-deception,
> waiting for God Himself, in His own good time
> and after His own way, to draw it upwards, since
> all prayer is His own free gift, and due to nothing
> of our own. Self-abasement brings the vivid
> realisation of faith, contrition brings the truest
> love, self-oblation brings union : and, with these
> secured, what will the good God not do ? '
> (p. 189).

   .    .    .     .    .

For some years he had known that his fainting
fits were a serious symptom and that his trouble was
*angina pectoris*. Five or six years before his death he
had seen a heart specialist on one of his visits to
London from Teignmouth, and he reported the
authoritative diagnosis with his familiar twisted
smile. ' I do not know when the end will come,'

he said. ' You can go on for quite a long time with
angina. It may come suddenly. I have a great
deal to do ; but it is all in God's hands.' The
diagnosis made no difference whatever to his life,
and he never referred to it again. The knowledge
of a possibly sudden ending only stimulated him to
make the most of the day that was left to him in
view of the coming night. Had he confined himself
to writing, he might have husbanded his strength
more. But he accepted engagements to preach,
lecture, give retreats, and attend church functions
just as though he were in perfect health. He hated
to refuse any appeal made to him, if it were at all
compatible with the work he was doing at Teignmouth. He had many attacks of pain. He was
sometimes surprised in them by a chance visitor to
his room ; but he never referred to them. To
outward appearance he seemed in good health and
showed little signs of age.

For the last year before his death the attacks were
more frequent and severe ; but they were passing,
and once the paroxysm was over he was instantly
his usual cheerful self. He feared to alarm his
friends, the more so as he knew that very little could
be done to remedy his condition. Some months
before the end he had had a severe attack when
climbing the hill to the Notre Dame convent at
Teignmouth. He rallied from it and went slowly
on to give his conference. Of his last days one of
the Benedictine nuns writes :

' The pain in his heart became much more
frequent ; formerly he needed much warmth,
but latterly he could not bear heat nor much bed-

clothes. On the morning of his death, as the Sister went to him for something, she found him leaning back, and he said : " What an old croaky I am getting ! " Our doctor comes every Monday and the Sister insisted on his seeing his Grace. . . . He seemed to have had some foreboding of his death. Other years, towards the end of his retreat (which he always made in Lent, and a very vigorous retreat too—strict silence) he was inclined to get a little depressed. This year, however, he was unusually bright and full of life and joyousness. But two days after he came out of retreat—that would be about six days before his death—he said to our chaplain, Provost Burns, during lunch : " I shall not be here much longer." The Provost answered : " You must not talk like this," and they made a few jokes and passed on to other themes of conversation.

The last time he was in London, February 2–11, he saw an unusual number of old friends. It proved to be the last good-bye visit.'

Another writes as follows :

' On Monday morning, the day of his death, he said Mass as usual, took Holy Communion to the sick, and gave us Holy Communion. Some Sisters afterwards remarked that they had noticed he had been slower than usual and did not seem quite well. He had lunch with our chaplain, and was bright and making jokes when they went upstairs. The Provost then left for Plymouth to attend Chapter on Tuesday, and the Archbishop was to supply for him at Benediction. Between

2.0 and 3.0 he went into the garden for his usual half-hour walk, saying his Office. He then saw a Sister who had wished to speak to him. At 3.0 a missionary priest came to see him and they talked in his room for half an hour. The Archbishop then took him to the chapel where he left him. In returning he had reached the corridor in the priest's house, when a Sister working not far off heard a heavy fall. She rushed to the Archbishop who had first fallen forward against a door and then right on his back. A second Sister came, and they lifted him up. He gasped for breath but was unconscious. They quickly fetched the priest from the chapel and another priest who had brought him in his motor. They anointed his Grace. He was already dead.'

A solemn Requiem was sung by the Bishop of Plymouth at the convent on Thursday morning in the presence of many members of the Cathedral Chapter, the Abbot of Downside, and many other priests. The Requiem at Farm Street was sung by Archbishop Godfrey, the Apostolic Delegate ; after which the Archbishop was buried in the cemetery attached to Manresa House, Roehampton, where his priestly work had begun and his young manhood taken its life's impress.

The last section of his lecture on the Unitive Way is entitled ' The Mystic.' In it the Archbishop has perhaps come as near to self-portraiture as in anything he ever wrote. That he is wholly unconscious of it does not affect the fidelity of the picture. He had read much in all the approved authors on

D

Mystical Theology.  He had doubtless from time to time encountered men or women in whom he recognised the genuine mystic spirit.  But it was his own experience which gave so sure a touch to his firm and unhesitating guidance of others in the higher and more difficult ways of the spiritual life. Without such experience books are of little avail and can produce but a notional assent to their teaching.  Even personal contacts with this type of spiritual life can be meaningless or unintelligible, the more so as it so often leaves the soul incapable of explaining itself in ordinary human speech. All the mystics from St. Paul onwards are unanimous about this.  Readers of St. Teresa will recall how she almost wearies by her continued insistence on the point.  That the Archbishop should have understood so profoundly and have recognised so uniformly the genuine mystic when he encountered him is surely an indication of some such spirit in his own life. A careful reading of his *Ascetical and Mystical Theology* shows him in this light.  Thus he can write :

> ' The true mystic is always naturally as well as supernaturally humble.  He fears nothing more than publicity, for somehow all publicity seems to him all awry.  He shivers at honour paid to him, for it is paid for that which to him matters nothing at all.  He hesitates to speak, because the things of which he would speak tie his tongue ; more often than not he does not know himself what it is he wishes to say, or how he may say it, or what will be its effect when it has been said. . . . He is haunted with the sense of his own foolishness and failure ' (pp. 205–6).

And again :

' Nevertheless, with all his inner fear and darkness, with all his outward ungainliness, and his
inability to adapt himself to other men, the true
mystic is utterly genuine and simple. . . . In his
simplicity he is always too prompt to say " yes "
and " no," only to discover that, more often, it
would have been better to have said neither.
Thus is he found guilty, in all sorts of ways, of
lack of worldly wisdom ; he will often make
mistakes, he is easily deceived, his longer vision
makes him unwise in his immediate generation,
and the consequences come back upon him.
But neither does this distress him ; he sees himself
as he is, and accounts himself worth nothing
more ' (p. 206).

And finally :

' He has learnt that the life he lives is a very
little thing, that truly it is not life but a walking
blindfold, that it is but a shadow of the great
reality, an imprisonment of the spirit that yearns
to be free, a mere entombment in " the body of
this death," with all its trappings and burthens.
He has discovered, and he marvels how others
fail to make the same discovery, that even in this
narrow world there is a life to be lived, far more
full than anything the world has to offer, that
there are ambitions more worthy of a man than
any little crowns or ribbons ; and he is straitened
until the baptism with which he must now be
baptised is accomplished. He is the most
unhappy of men, yet he is the happiest. . . .

So he is torn within himself, between joy and agony, between life and death ; and that while his ordinary life runs its course. He reads for relief, for guidance, authors whose souls are akin to his own ; he learns from them only that the way along which he is being led is a way of contradiction. They warn him that trouble will come upon him ; false accusation, misunderstanding, mere thoughtless cruelty, failure in his task, injustice, abuse, treachery, a breakdown in health ; in one way or another God will nail him to his cross, will test his love as gold in the furnace, will give him those signal proofs of His special care for him. To many his will seem a wasted life, a misfit, an aimless wandering only to be left to drift ; yet all the time he will know that he is following the star through the desert, that if he would be true to himself he can do no otherwise, that somewhere, somehow, he will come to Bethlehem, though it be through the hands of tyrants and the wiles of Pharisees. . . . He longs, almost only, to pray, though he knows not what he asks for when he prays ; to pray more and still more, yet the more he prays and the more he lives in prayer, the more it seems to him that he knows nothing about it. He reaches out to the infinite, till time and space, and all they contain, either vanish to nothing, or are pressed into a passing instant ; yet the nearer he seems to reach his goal, the farther it recedes from him. He apprehends a little, and the curtain falls ; he touches it, and it is no longer there. There comes a time when, as it were, he is lost in space between earth and heaven. He has leapt from

off the earth, his feet are no longer on solid
ground, yet his hands have failed to grasp the
battlements of the eternal city, and he falls back,
even as a lost soul, through the impenetrable
darkness. . . . One day the sun shines again,
and he finds he is falling not through darkness,
but through the infinite light. He reaches out
once more and grasps, not a truth, but the very
Truth itself. He presses it to his heart, and is not
distressed any more when he finds it but a
shadow; for truth embraced reveals to him yet
greater truth, leading ever upward to that substantial infinite Truth, with which alone he can
be satisfied : *Lux vera, satietas plena, gaudium
sempiternum, iucunditas consummata, felicitas perfecta*'
(pp. 207–9).

Such is the Archbishop's unconscious portrait
of himself. Those who knew him best, especially
those who knew him from within, will have no
difficulty in recognising the likeness. At St. Mary's,
Chelsea, ' his first expressed wish was for an oratory
where he could retire for meditation and prayer.'
At Teignmouth ' The Archbishop had been accustomed to spend an hour from nine to ten p.m. in
prayer in our chapel. He scarcely seemed to move.
We just heard him very gently opening the door to
go away, but not another sound.' In India it is
told of him that he spent hours in prayer before the
Blessed Sacrament. He more than once admitted
that he did not find prayer easy, that he felt he was
getting nowhere in it. He knew too much to be
disturbed at such apparent failure, nor did it ever
cause him to relax his efforts. His life almost from

the day of his consecration as Archbishop was one
of suffering, in India, in London, and finally at
Teignmouth where he suffered from the very
fact that he was suffering ; for he shrank intensely
from giving trouble or being a burden to others,
a shrinking which no assurance to the contrary
could altogether remove. Yet, could he have
commented dispassionately on his own life, he
would have recognised it as but following the
authentic lines of all the great and generous with
God, with its double transfiguration on Thabor and
on Calvary.

From his Stonyhurst days he had known the
taste of success—in power, subtle influence with
others, ability in self-expression. He had been
acclaimed a great teacher alike in literature and
in the things of the spirit. His elevation to the
episcopate, though not of his seeking, was an added
testimony to the high esteem in which he was held
by those best fitted to judge. With all this he was
the humblest, most self-effacing of men. And with
it all from the day of his consecration went the
shadow of the cross. As he himself says, from his
reading he knew that trouble must come upon him,
misunderstanding, mere thoughtless cruelty, failure
in his task, a breakdown in health. Those who knew
him best could comment at length on each of these
words. For the time being he was blind to the
immense service he was rendering, perhaps because
he was too acutely conscious of the truth of New-
man's saying that all good is done at the cost of him
who does it. On his return to England it seemed to
him that ' his was a wasted life, a misfit, an aimless
wandering only to be left to drift.' Yet all the time

he knew that he was following the star and that he would somewhere, somehow, come to Bethlehem in the end. He was at once the most unhappy of men, yet he was the happiest ; for he was, though altogether without cause as it seemed to most, ' haunted with the sense of his own foolishness and failure.'

With this suffering there undoubtedly went much external success. Not even he could be blind to the fact that he was liked ; that his retreats, his preaching, his books were looked forward to ; that many sought eagerly for and felt safe in his guidance. But to him such things mattered little. What mattered supremely was his discovery that ' even in this narrow world there is a life to be lived, far more full than anything the world has to offer,' and he ' was straitened until the baptism with which he must now be baptised was accomplished.' In his increasing weakness and paroxysms of pain, in the felt slowing down of the tempo of life and its passage into the shadows he recognised that ' God was nailing him to his cross and testing his love as gold in the furnace.' Earlier in his lectures he had spoken of the intertwining of the purgative and unitive ways, and the thought may well have been prompted by life as he actually found it, that ' entombment in the body of this death with all its trappings and burthens.' At last he has reached out and grasped, not a truth, but the very Truth itself, even that substantial infinite Truth with which alone he can be satisfied—*Lux vera, satietas plena.* Like another great lover he has passed *Ex umbris et imaginibus in veritatem.*

# EDITOR'S NOTE

THE present work discusses the question of 'Ignatian Prayer.' In his monumental *Histoire du Sentiment Religieux en France*, Vol. III, H. Bremond had drawn a sharp distinction between the supposed 'method' of St. Ignatius and that of the French school as represented by Cardinal de Bérulle, de Condren, and his disciple M. Olier, the saintly founder of Saint-Sulpice. Without going into the controversy the Archbishop here seeks to show that the teaching of St. Ignatius Loyola on prayer—even that part of it contained in the brief notes which make up the *Spiritual Exercises*—has been much misunderstood and misrepresented by casual readers, and even by casual commentators; and that so far from its being a mere insistence on so-called 'discursive' prayer it is the teaching of an authentic contemplative for whom the whole meaning of prayer is the direct contact of the soul with God.

It would seem that the book was left unfinished at the author's death. Many blank pages remain, and though he has written a 'Conclusion,' it is detached from the rest of the MS. as if its place in the pagination had not yet been determined.

# CONTENTS

# AUTHOR'S PREFACE

THE purpose of this study is not in any way to describe or develop the Spiritual Exercises of St. Ignatius ; that has been done many times during the course of four hundred years, and, besides, is done more or less in every retreat that is made under their guidance. Its purpose rather is, if one can, by means of the Book of the Exercises alone, to detect the mind of its author in regard to prayer. So much is assumed, and loosely written, concerning St. Ignatius Loyola and prayer ; so much that seems to contradict what, from other evidence, is certain concerning him. There is ascribed to him a ' method ' of prayer, so peculiarly his own that it goes by his name only ; from that ' method ' there is attributed to him a concept of prayer that is said to be different from the accepted tradition till his time. It is more than insinuated that, thanks to him, not necessarily in disapproval of him, there have grown up two different ' schools ' of prayer in the Church. For the most part those who make this assumption have never read the Book of the Spiritual Exercises, much less have they given it the month's attention which a right understanding of it demands.

They will say that there is now no need to make the Exercises in order to understand the book. The assumption is now so commonly accepted, even by members of the Society of Jesus, and even in their own spiritual books, that there can be no necessity to go any further. St. Ignatius Loyola, so everyone agrees, was by nature and training a soldier, out for the conquest of the world for Christ, and he adapted the spiritual life to this end. He was a man of one idea, the making of a spiritual army, and all other purposes were only of secondary account. This Book of the Spiritual Exercises was a kind of military text-book, a soldier's manual written for the training of a soldier, and that the concept of prayer described in it was adapted to that end. Though the soldier's virtue, obedience, is scarcely mentioned in the Exercises, though the Director is warned against imposing his will in any way, though later, in the Constitutions, when St. Ignatius describes his ideal follower, the virtue of obedience does not appear, though in his famous Letter on Obedience he expressly excludes the obedience of the soldier, still the assumption continues. The system he established was very splendid; it has produced the most wonderful results; no one wishes to diminish the glory of the saint, or of the Order he founded; still it was fundamentally different from what had been before. One may go to St. Ignatius to be ' drilled ' in sanctity; one would not go to him to be trained in prayer. St. Ignatius is a saint of action, full of sacrifice and zeal; he is not a saint from whom the contemplative has much to learn.

Such is a common view held of the spirituality of St. Ignatius. And yet when we look at the man himself, in the grotto at Manresa, with all the panoply of a soldier deliberately laid aside, in the streets of Jerusalem, seeking to be forgotten and ignored, in prison at Alcala and Salamanca, influencing people about him till they wanted to become Carthusians, at times, it would seem, doubting whether he should become one himself, waiting almost twenty years before he set himself to any definite task, we feel that there is some contradiction between the man and the theory of the spiritual life attributed to him. Out of forty-five years he had been a soldier for barely five, and that, for the most part, more for the love and excitement of the thing than as a serious profession ; he was scarcely a soldier in the modern sense of the word. When, further, we find his immediate disciples, no matter where they went or what was the work they did, yet more conspicuous for their prayer, and even their ecstasies, Blessed Peter Faber, St. Francis Xavier, St. Francis Borgia, and others, we cannot help wondering whether his teaching on prayer can have been such as it is described and, as such, dismissed. When, in the next generation, we find some of the greatest contemplatives enthusiastic in his praise, St. Philip Neri, St. Charles Borromeo, St. Teresa of Avila, St. Mary Magdalen de Pazzi, to mention only these, we become sure that there was more in his training in prayer than the mere making of spiritual soldiers. When, lastly, we see the long line of ' contemplative ' writers which has stretched down from his own generation to ours, all sons of the saint and trained entirely on the Spiritual Exercises, we can have no further doubt that the summary assumption we have mentioned must contain an inherent fallacy. Since these are its results, the teaching of St. Ignatius cannot be very different

from that of other masters of the spiritual life ;
since the Book of the Exercises was treasured by
contemplatives not merely as much as, but even
more than, by apostles, it cannot have been written
for the training of spiritual soldiers only.   For
spiritual soldiers, yes ;  but not in the first place,
and not for them alone.

In other words there are here, apparently, two
concepts of the saint and his book, and of his attitude to the spiritual life, which are incompatible.
Which of them is true ?   Or if both are true, can
they be reconciled ?   It is with the object of trying
to answer these questions that the present study
has been undertaken.   What was really the mind
of St. Ignatius in regard to prayer, not so much as
he practised it himself, but as he taught it to
others ?   By discovering this, concealed beneath,
rather than revealed in, his training of the perfect
man, we may hope to solve the problem of the
undoubted mystic who, nevertheless, founded the
Order of the Companions of Jesus.

But before we begin it will be well to make one
remark.   The Book of the Spiritual Exercises is not
a book as we ordinarily understand the word ;  it
is merely a collection of notes for guidance, and
those notes, at times, would seem to a modern
student to have been clumsily put together.   They
assume from beginning to end that he who reads
them knows how to interpret them ;  he has already
been initiated into the Exercises themselves.   There
are Annotations, and Additions, and other head-
ings, leading to further subdivisions, thrown
together in such a way that no modern publisher
would dream of publishing them as a book.   There

are arrangements of meditations which would suggest that something has been lost. For instance,
after dividing his ' book,' not into chapters but into
' weeks,' the first week is found to have only one
' day ' in it, with no suggestion for any more ; the
fourth ' week ' gives only one meditation, and
leaves us to do the rest for ourselves. We are con-
tinually being drawn aside from our main purpose
by other considerations ; sometimes by apparently
petty details such as the light in the room, sometimes by what are called ' rules,' about such things
as eating, giving alms, and thinking in the mind
of the Church. Seldom, we may say never, is a
meditation given elaborately enough for a beginner
in mental prayer ; all assume that someone will
explain them. To a casual reader the book cannot
but appear to be a jumble, and to contain nothing
new ; no one could possibly take it as a book for
spiritual reading, as one takes, let us say, *The
Imitation of Christ.*

All this is true ; as a book the Spiritual Exercises
must take a low place ; had St. Ignatius lived in
our time perhaps even he would have yielded to
the modern spirit and arranged his material differently. At first one might wonder whether, with
his peculiar education, St. Ignatius was capable of
writing a book in the ordinary meaning of the
word ; but this is answered by the only other
complete book we have from him, the Constitutions of the Society of Jesus, which is a masterpiece
of right order, divided into definite chapters, with
elaborate footnotes, worthy to be compared with
any modern thesis. Moreover, whatever were his
own capabilities, he had about him, as secretaries

E

and advisers, men of the best university training ; and St. Ignatius was always willing to learn. The truth would rather seem to be that the form of the book was deliberate ; it was never intended to be printed, but was meant 'for private circulation only.' He himself gave the Exercises to others according to these notes ; he intended that they, in turn, should give them to a wider audience ; for these, who had already gone through them, he wrote down these notes, drawn from his own experience, pointing out details to which they should attend, and which they would interpret from a like experience of their own. In other words the book was written, not to help exercitants to make retreats, but for those who had already made them and were to give them to others. This is specially noticeable at the beginning, and when he gives directions as to the different treatment of different kinds of souls. Unless one has already gone through the retreat, they seem to say, they are unintelligible, and no amount of mere study will catch the meaning that lies beneath them. It is with the Spiritual Exercises as it is with the Gospels. One may read the latter and never catch their real content, the portrait of Christ, the Son of God ; one may read the Book of the Exercises and never grasp the mind of the author, or the special object he has in view.

It is to our purpose to call attention to this at the outset because it is the significance of his assumptions that most reveal the mind of the saint. We may say that in the book he teaches almost nothing, but takes much for granted ; and it is the aim of this study to examine those assumptions and see what they imply. There is no wish to elaborate the Exercises themselves; it is the author himself whom we seek, and the truth of life as he saw it, and described it to his followers. In doing this we deliberately confine ourselves to the Book of the Exercises alone, though it is by no means the only place in which St. Ignatius may be discovered; whatever else may be added we reserve for notes and appendices.

# I

# INTRODUCTION : THE AUTHOR AND THE BOOK

THE question has often been asked, and many attempts have been made in recent years to answer it, whether and to what extent the Book of the Spiritual Exercises of St. Ignatius depends on other works. It may be taken for granted that no author, especially one who writes on spiritual subjects, is wholly and entirely original. He must depend, at least for his inspiration, often also for his material, on those who have gone before him ; who have learnt from their own study and experience, and have written their lessons down. His originality will almost always consist in confirming and adapting what they have written to his own circumstances, thus giving that material a new setting, a new expression, a new object, perhaps even a new life. Though there is little room for originality in spiritual literature, there is, in its application, an almost infinite variety. Now Inigo Loyola, the raw recruit in the service of God at the age of thirty-one, can have been no exception to this rule. He began his new spiritual life with almost no spiritual learning, and for his first spiritual ideas, apart from the light and grace of God, had need to depend on what he read, or what he was taught. We may say this with all the

greater confidence because no saint has ever been
more careful, both for himself and in the training
of others, to insist on following the tradition of the
Church. The very last entry in the Book of the
Exercises is sufficient illustration of this. When
he has finished his work, and has trained his exercitant to the best he can make of him, he gives him
as a parting gift a set of rules :

> ' For the true feeling which we ought to have
> in the Church militant,'

rules, as they are usually called, ' for thinking with
the Church,' which are almost disconcerting in
their detail.

For whatever else Inigo Loyola had in his
composition, he had begun with the traditional
Basque faith which nothing could shake. He
might have failed in practice, like others of his
kind, he might have had no better record than
other men. Nevertheless, like them, if ever there
had been question of insult to the faith of his
forefathers, he would have fought for it, and died
for it, without a moment's hesitation. Such, with
perhaps little more in his spiritual development,
unless it was a deep devotion to the Mother of
God, was the man who lay on his bed, convalescent
and restless, after his wound at Pampeluna. To
while away the time, he was forced to read the only
books that could be found for him. One was the
*Flos Sanctorum*, a collection of lives and stories of
saints ; the other was the *Vita Christi*, by the
Carthusian, who had once been a Dominican,
Ludolph of Saxony. Later, when Inigo lived at
Manresa, it is known that he had in his possession

*The Imitation of Christ.* The impression made by these three books was deep and lasting ; on them, along with the New Testament, so far as books could provide it, the first foundation of the Book of the Exercises was laid. Perhaps it is in grateful recognition of this that at one stage of the Exercises the author writes :

> ' For the second week, and so for all the future, it profits much to read at times in the books of *The Imitation of Christ*, or in the Gospels, or from Lives of the Saints.'

But besides books, there were other spiritual influences which Inigo sought and found in his first days. Those were the Benedictines at Montserrat, where he completed his first surrender, made his General Confession, hung up his sword, and definitely began again. It is possible, even probable, that here he became acquainted with the *Spiritual Exercises* of the Benedictine, Cisneros ; though a comparison of this book with that of Ignatius shows little resemblance between them except in name. There were, next, the Dominican fathers at Manresa, who seem from the first to have recognised and fostered the sanctity of the extraordinary mendicant who came among them ; Inigo always knew he had a welcome at their convent ; and, if he wished for it, a home. There was the Cistercian, Alfonso de Guerreto, whom Inigo took for his confessor during his extraordinary life at Manresa, and with whom at one time he had proposed to himself to make his permanent home. The influence of Alfonso must have been very great. Inigo had come to Manresa, intending to stay but a few days ; in fact he stayed the greater part of a year.  During that period he went through every kind of spiritual experience, from diabolical visitations and scruples to the highest ecstasy ; through them all he was directed mainly by the Cistercian, to whom he submitted in utter obedience.  It would seem, then, that from him he learnt at least the first principles of those Rules of Discernment which, in many ways, most reveal the mind of the saint in his maturity.

Thus in the providence of God St. Benedict, St. Bernard, St. Bruno, and St. Dominic contributed materially, from the very beginning, to the making of St. Ignatius.  There can be little doubt that a passage in Ludolph inspired his pilgrimage to the Holy Land, that he might begin his new life of likeness to Christ by seeing for himself and treading the very ground his Ideal had trod.  On his return Inigo settled first at Barcelona.  There he took for his confessor a Franciscan, fray Diégo de Alcantara, and from him imbibed the spirit of St. Francis and St. Bonaventure, three at least of whose works, or of works attributed to him, left on him a permanent impression.  But we learn from Polanco that, while at Barcelona, he came across another book which it is important to notice.  This was the *Institutio Militis Christiani*, by Erasmus.  It is recorded that he did not like the book ; Erasmus was one of those authors whom, later, he was to exclude from the curriculum of his students.  Nevertheless, there would seem to be good ground to believe that the work of Erasmus gave him the idea of two of his most famous meditations, the Kingdom of Christ and the Two Standards.  If this is true, then the myth of the 'soldier saint' becomes yet more remote. From Barcelona Inigo went to Alcala. There he stayed with one Diégo de Eguia. Now Diégo was the brother of a printer who had produced from his press two books, *The Mirror of Illustrious Persons* and *The Art of Serving God*, by a Franciscan, fray Alonso de Madrid. There are passages in both of these books which would seem to make it certain that the author of the Spiritual Exercises had studied them to good account.

Indeed, during all these early days, one gets the impression, that while Inigo lost no opportunity of teaching and influencing others to better things, yet he was always on the look-out to learn from any who might help him, or keep him in conformity with those who had gone before him. This could not but have been the more impressed upon him by the suspicion under which he lived, both at Alcala and at Salamanca. In both places he fell into the hands of the Inquisition ; and though in his various trials nothing could be charged against him, still the experience taught him how careful he must needs be to beware of novelty, above all in the matter of prayer, if he would be free to do the good he was longing to do among his fellow-men. But he had meanwhile learnt something more. From Spain he went to Paris, and here one seems to notice a great change. He had learnt in the three Spanish cities that if he would himself make the progress he needed to become a guide for others he must give himself more to his philosophical and theological studies ; prayer alone was not enough. He had also learnt, from failures and disappointments in three cities, how he might

put to better account his course of Exercises, such
as they then were.   With one exception it would,
perhaps, be difficult to find in his book any direct
influence from his reading in Paris ;   probably it
was most affected by his courses in philosophy and
theology, pursued under the Dominican fathers in
the Rue Saint-Jacques.

But one influence made a lasting impression.   In
the university of Paris during his time Humanism
tending to atheistic rationalism was rampant ;
morality among the undergraduates was at a very
low ebb indeed ;   Lutheranism, the new thing
imported from Germany, with its specious cham-
pioning of individual liberty, was a matter of
debate, with some it was a mark of the new intel-
lectualism and the new life.   Calvin was a student
in Paris at this very time ;   it is possible that he
attended the same lectures as Inigo Loyola.   On
the other hand, as always in like conditions, there
was, and there had always been, a strong group of
serious seekers for reform among both students and
professors ;   and these had been, and were still
being, influenced by the Brothers of the Common
Life, from Windesheim in Holland.   Gerson, one
of these Brothers, had once been Chancellor of the
University, and his memory was not dead.   These
Brothers, though devoted to education as the true
method of reform, nevertheless combined with it
a steady attention to prayer.   They revised prayer,
so to speak, in such a way as to adapt it more to
the needs of the student.   On this account they
had brought into the university a new kind of
spiritual book, including such as the works of
Ramon Lull and Ruysbroeck, but also many

written by the Brothers themselves. Above all
things else they were practical ; while they encouraged every kind of intellectual pursuit they also
aimed at making the perfect man ; while they put
prayer in the front of their system, they also taught
it in a way that it might influence, and not be
divorced from, the life of thinking and aspiring
men. That Inigo, the lover of *The Imitation of
Christ*, the masterpiece of the Brothers of the Common Life, came under their guidance is certain ;
we have only to compare his so-called ' method '
with that of the Brothers, handed down from
generation to generation.

Such would seem to be some of the chief spiritual
influences brought to bear on the author of the
Book of the Exercises, during his period of training
from Pampeluna to Paris, a period of fourteen years,
and during which time the Book was being
developed. Inigo Loyola was no wide reader, as
can be easily understood ; he was content with a
little at a time, so long as it led him to a solid conviction. Moreover, he was not a man of many
ideas ; Laynez, one of his disciples, and his successor as General of the Society of Jesus, who knew
him as well as did anyone, sums him up by saying
that he was a man of few virtues, but that he made
those virtues sink very deep. It was during all
this time that the Book of the Exercises grew. The
core, as it were, came to him at Manresa ; but for
the rest, to quote the saint's own words, recorded
by one who asked him :

' The Exercises were not written all at one
time. Whatever I noticed to have been useful

to myself I put down regularly in writing, because it seemed to me that it might also be useful to others ; for instance, the method of the particular examen.'

And such in fact is the Book, bearing upon itself many indications that it has been a growth. It is a collection of notes, gathered together, emended, rearranged for the benefit of others, but with many connecting links omitted, left for him to insert who has already learnt their use. They are the fruit of one man's own experiences in the course of fourteen years and more, and that man Inigo Loyola ; whom no man surpassed in the romantic ambition of youth, who, when he found himself, turned that ambition to the discovery of the absolute truth and nothing else, who, once he saw his goal, would brook no obstacle to its attainment. He had begun his new life, at the mature age of thirty-one, on a bed of suffering, where, in a crude way at first, under the influence of Christ and the followers of Christ he had found a nobler object to live for and had made up his mind to live for it. He had not yet seen very far ; only, perhaps, that this new life, if it was to be quite genuine, must begin with utter cleanness of heart, with a general confession, a shunning of all sin, and a safeguarding of himself from it for the future. This he had done at Montserrat. But soon he had learnt that this was not enough ; there was still the old man within him, there were still temptations to be overcome, it was still needful to control himself, to measure his steps, to fix his route, its beginning and its end, to teach himself how to grow in prayer. At times there would be excess, and it would need to be curbed ; at times he would find his soul empty and sluggish, and it would need to be fed and urged.  But above all that the soul might grow in love it must also grow in knowledge ;  for no one can love what he does not know.  It must grow in knowledge of itself, in knowledge of Christ, in knowledge of God and of the love of God ;  all this he learnt from Ludolph, from the confessors who guided him, from his own experience.

Such was the process that went on in the grotto at Manresa.  Whither it was leading we have no reason to believe that he knew ;  it was still eighteen years before he founded his Order, and many gropings and failures came between.  But whatever his work in life was to be, there was another and a more definite goal that held his gaze ;  what that goal was, the prolonged ecstasies in the cave at Manresa indicate clearly enough.  Already this cripple from the battlefield had gone far in the way of the mystic saints ;  he had joined the ranks of the highest contemplatives.  As yet there was little indication of the apostle, of the man of action, unless it be that even at Manresa he would ' go about doing good,' as must every soul, contemplative or active, who has the love of God burning within him.  And yet, even at this stage, when he himself hesitates whether to adopt the life of the contemplative, when he has no thought of making apostles, he tells us that the core of the Exercises was composed.  They had grown with his growth, and, so far, they had only ended here ;  they had begun with the Carthusian, Ludolph, and had ended with the Cistercian, Alfonso, and for a time it seemed that there they would remain.  To this goal the Spiritual Exercises, in their first form, tended, and we know that for the rest of his life they were never substantially altered.  Much was added to them, but we can scarcely doubt that underneath all additions there was never lost the contemplative, even the mystic, ideal which their author, to use his own frequent phrase, ' had learnt at Manresa.'

And yet, during all this time and after, Inigo could not but remain master of himself ;  he was still the independent hidalgo, making his own way, though he already saw that this would not be for always.  If there is anything characteristic of him it is this ;  perhaps it is what critics mean who speak of him as different from other spiritual leaders. Though there is little, if anything, in his Book which may not be traced to an earlier source, though he was conspicuous in his desire to learn from his spiritual guides, still he seemed to take nothing ' on faith ' ;  he tested what he learnt upon himself, and according to the result accepted it or set it aside.  In the Book of the Exercises there are countless echoes of Ludolph, of *The Imitation of Christ*, but there are no quotations ;  there is nothing that could even be taken for a quotation. Everything is Inigo's own.  He has read and studied deeply till the matter has sunk deep into his mind ; he has then gone to his prayer and seen the result ; then he has written down what that experience has taught him, not merely what he has learnt ;  even from the best of guides.  And the same is true, perhaps even more true, of the later years of training. In Paris, much as he came under the influence of

the Brothers of the Common Life, yet the evidences
of that influence, in detail at least, are even less
than are those of Ludolph.   It is rather, as it were,
on the broader field that it may be seen ;  in the
trace of scholastic outlook when he treats of God
and man, in the effort to train the mind to greater
concentration that it may pray the better, in the
adjustment of perspective for the making of the
perfect man.

All this will, it is hoped, at least make it clear that
the Book of the Exercises is a book which cannot
merely be read ;  to do that alone not only would be
to miss its meaning, but to find in it no meaning at
all.   One can read Ludolph ;  his great work was
written to be read.   One can read the *Imitation*,
but not all at once ;  the more we read of it at any
one time the less we tend to understand it.   So is it
with other spiritual books ;  some are written to
be read, others to be pondered, and to expect to
fathom the latter by reading them is to do injustice
to the book, to the author, and, most of all, to oneself.   No man is so able as to pierce with a glance
the mind of another, not even the mind of a fool ;
much less the mind of one who has pondered for
years over a line which, at last, he has thought fit to
write.   And such are the lines which make up this
baffling, and in many ways disconcerting, book.
For it goes beyond even the *Imitation*.   That book
at least is in order ;  it has been written that it
might be read, though it be only a little at a time.
The Book of the Exercises has been written, not
that it might be read, but that at every step it might
be set aside and put into practice.   It has been
written with the understanding that he who used it

had by his side an interpreter who would explain it to him. It expects that its study will occupy thirty days, not less ; this tiny book, less in size than the *Imitation*. It asks him who uses it not only to do so unprejudiced, but even to feel kindly towards it ; not only to be ready to point out its peculiarities, and differences from other books, but rather to see where they agree. Even St. Ignatius foresaw the opposition he was likely to arouse ; he foresaw it because he had already experienced and felt it. This is the significance of the note with which, after the introductory Annotations, the book begins :

> ' In order that both he who gives the spiritual exercises as well as he who receives them may be the more helped and benefited, it must be presupposed that every good Christian ought to be more ready to justify his neighbour's statement than to condemn it. And if he cannot justify it, let him ask how he understands it, and if he understands it in a wrong sense, correct him with love. And if that does not suffice, let him still seek all suitable means that the statement may receive a good sense and be justified.'

Such a ' preface ' tells its own tale. It is customary for prefaces to be written after the rest of the work is finished ; in this case, clearly, it has followed long years of use and experience. But St. Ignatius Loyola knew that though superficial readers might pretend to put him in the wrong the deeper men of prayer would find that he was right ; that he was one with those who had gone before him, that he put no hindrance to the very highest contemplation, that his perfect man was, above all things else, so far above all else that the rest was a mere sequence, a man of prayer. To this end, aware of the suspicion under which he wrote, it is again characteristic of him that he concentrated all his energies on the perfecting of this one book which, nevertheless, was not a book. We may regret, in our more book-ridden day, that he did not give us a more finished and better-ordered work ; still there is one experience which makes us doubt whether we would have been any better off. Hundreds, probably thousands, of attempts have been made to re-write the Exercises in better order ; hundreds of volumes have been published, bearing the title, ' The Spiritual Exercises of St. Ignatius,' most, but not all, written by his own disciples. Yet not one of these hundreds or thousands, no matter how great or holy its author, has been able to supersede the original. Some, for clearness' sake, have added to it, and the addition is at once felt to be the author's own ; excellent it may be, but seldom St. Ignatius. Others have subtracted from the book an apparent non-essential ; at once the understanding reader feels that something has been lost. It is this which makes one realise that though to us the book looks unfinished, yet to the author it was as perfect a work as he could make it. Beginning with the outline written at Manresa, going out to teach other men the way he had found so useful for himself, we are told that he never ceased emending what he had written, altering a word here and there, adding more as experience of other men suggested. In Barcelona and Alcala he learnt enough to adapt to other souls what he had himself discovered for the ' Discernment of Spirits.' In Paris he was led

F

to add the ' Rules for thinking with the Church,' incorporating as they do the Acta et Decreta of the Provincial Council of Sens, published in Paris in 1529. It is likely, too, that he wrote in Paris the ' Rules for Alms-giving,' and the ' Rules for Temperance in Food.' For the first, his own experience during the last years, the abundance he gave away, the need to advise the men who gathered round him with regard to their own patrimony, made it advisable to lay down certain principles ; when one reads these Rules apart, one is convinced that some such occasion was their origin, and that only later were they added to the Exercises as something to be preserved. Nadal tells us that before Inigo left his first companions in Paris,

' after he had finished his own studies, he com-piled his first notes of exercises, added more, and unified them all.'

# II

# THE ANNOTATIONS: THE PLACE OF PRAYER

**B**EFORE any step is made in the Exercises, they begin with a series of preliminary remarks, called 'Annotations.' These 'Annotations' are intended, not for one who goes through the Exercises but for him who gives them; which of itself is sufficient indication of the purpose of the Book itself. But on this account, because they are directions to the director, they show the mind of the author with regard to prayer, perhaps better than anything else in the whole work. And here, first of all, it is important to notice that when he gives an introductory definition of his Book, 'Spiritual Exercises,' he gives it only in terms of prayer. Moreover, he includes in his definition every kind of prayer imaginable. Thus he begins (Annotation 1):

'By this title, "spiritual exercises," is to be understood every method of examining the conscience, of meditating, of contemplating, of vocal and mental prayer, and of other spiritual operations such as will be spoken of hereafter.'

Prayer, then, from the outset is primary and paramount. It occupies the first place, it persists all the

77

time ; whatever else the title may include will, he
says, ' be spoken of hereafter.' This is immediately
followed, in the same paragraph, by what may seem
to be virtually another definition. Though the next
sentence begins with ' For,' as if it were an explanation of the first, still its substance, and the terms used,
are altogether different : the ' spiritual exercises '
now become :

> ' All methods of preparing the soul to rid itself
> of all disordered affections, and, after having got
> rid of them, to seek and find the divine will in
> the disposition of one's life for the salvation of
> the soul, are called spiritual exercises.'

In other words, in the very first paragraph the
author joins together prayer and self-conquest,
prayer and the perfect fulfilment of the will of God,
in this sense at least, that the one cannot be without
the other. By prayer we learn best to subdue
ourselves, by subduing ourselves we learn best how
to pray ; already we have the key to the whole
spirituality of St. Ignatius. The perfect will of
God is the end, prayer is the means, both to discover it and to fulfil it ; and these two constitute
the operation of the spiritual life. The two are
complementary, equally necessary, both for the
end to be attained and for their own existence ;
self-conquest without prayer may lead to Stoicism
and thence to mere pride, prayer without self-
conquest to illuminism in its many forms. This is
no new doctrine. It is the repeated teaching and
practice of the Early Church, culminating in St.
Augustine against the Stoicism of Pelagius ; it is
the emphasised teaching of St. Peter of Alcantara

and Louis of Granada, of St. Teresa and St. John
of the Cross, against the false mysticism with which
they were surrounded, and which Ignatius himself
had long since learnt to fear.

In this first Annotation we already come across
the word ' contemplating ' ; it is at least interesting
to note that it occurs in the first sentence of the
Book of the Exercises.  In one form or another the
word ' contemplate,' ' contemplation,' etc., comes
in the book eighty-four times, more than once in
every two pages.   Nowhere is contemplation
defined, as it is not defined by other mystics ;
what it means it is left to the reader to gather,
sufficiently at least for the author's purpose.  In
one way, and perhaps in only one, the word is
differently used by St. Ignatius and St. Teresa.  The
former never uses it in that specialised sense, in
which it is sometimes used by the latter, to signify
a state of soul rather than a kind of prayer ; always
he understands it as an ' exercise,' though with
infinite consequences, as we shall see.  St. Teresa,
with her usual fluency and disregard of precise
terms, uses the word in both senses ; she uses it to
describe a state, partly because of the kind of
prayer prevalent in that state, partly because she
could find no more suitable word to express what
she wished to imply.   She speaks of the final
arriving, when prayer and life are one ; therefore
she uses the same word to cover both.   But St.
Ignatius has another purpose ; moreover, by nature
and training he is more exact.   Not only is he
the most careful of writers, weighing every word
as he writes, correcting and re-correcting, but
in his book he is expressly dealing with a soul

in another phase. St. Teresa is describing a
' state ' which has been reached ; St. Ignatius is
training a soul towards that state by means of
' exercises.' The ' state ' described by St. Teresa,
as she often points out when she writes for the
guidance of her novices, presupposes the ' exercise '
of contemplation described by St. Ignatius ; indeed,
in her teaching of prayer as such, as seen especially
in her book written for novices, *The Way of Perfection*, it is the ' exercise ' and not the ' state ' which
chiefly concerns her. But in the same way, as St.
Teresa assumes the ' exercise ' before the ' state,'
so St. Ignatius assumes that the ' state ' will follow
the ' exercise ' ; of this we hope to have many
proofs in the course of our study.

At once, as if the saint were conscious of the
importance of the word he has used, perhaps
nowhere is the principle of ' contemplation,' even
as St. Teresa understands it, more clearly laid
down than in the next paragraph, the second
Annotation. Here we must notice a peculiar
mannerism of style in all the writings of St. Ignatius.
He has a constant habit, scarcely ever failing to
seize an occasion, of coupling two words together
with an ' and ' or an ' or ' ; words which seldom
express quite the same thing, but nevertheless suggest one another and are complementary. Thus
in the first sentence of this Annotation he speaks
of ' meditating or contemplating,' and then, before
the sentence is completed, of ' contemplation or
meditation.' He says :

' The person who gives to another the method
and order [first couplet] for meditating or con-

templating [second couplet] should narrate faithfully the history for such a contemplation or
meditation [third couplet], going through the
points with merely a brief or summary [fourth
couplet] account.'

Now the ' or ' may imply a difference (Latin,
*aut*) or it may only suggest a synonym (Latin, *vel*) ;
and the fact that, in the sentence just quoted, the
order of the words is inverted might show that the
second is intended. In matter of fact it is not easy
to distinguish between the two words as St. Ignatius
used them ; and one gets the impression that he
was somewhat indifferent which word were used.
One almost hears him say : ' So long as you pray,
you may call it what you like, meditation or contemplation.' It is true the word ' meditation ' is
more common in the first part of the book, and
' contemplation ' is almost universal in the second.
Nevertheless, to define ' meditation ' as referring
to the method of the ' exercises ' of the First Week,
on Sin and its concomitants, and ' contemplation '
to the rest, is wholly incorrect, at least according
to the mind of the saint. He himself speaks of
' contemplating ' sin, and in the Additions or
Advices on prayer, before he has yet come to the
Second Week, he again uses the couplet, ' contemplation or meditation,' in reference to the First
Week alone. But before we attempt to define the
meaning of the word, or estimate its scope, let us
look at the rest of this Second Annotation, for it is
one of the most enlightening passages in the whole
book. After having warned him who gives the
points for ' meditation or contemplation ' that he

must give them exactly but not elaborately, the saint goes on :

'For the person who contemplates, taking the true foundation of the history, and going through it and reasoning for himself, if he discovers anything that explains or brings it home to him a little better, either by his own reasoning or in so far as his intellect is enlightened by the divine power, will find more relish and spiritual fruit therein than if he who is giving the exercises had amply explained and drawn out the meaning of the history. For it is not the abundance of knowledge that fills and satisfies the soul, but to feel and relish things interiorly.'

From this we learn several things :

(1) That he who makes the ' meditation or contemplation' must go through the matter independently for himself. It is not enough merely to repeat the points that have been given to him ; in some way the work must be his own.

(2) That his purpose must be, not to learn more, but to ' bring it home a little better,' as a living, practical truth.

(3) That by so doing, though he may miss much that has been said, still he will gain the true fruit of prayer.

(4) That the true fruit of prayer is not greater knowledge, but greater ' interior' realisation of a truth.

(5) Finally, and this is most important of all, fundamental to the whole of the teaching of St. Ignatius on prayer, that this ' interior' realisation will be gained in one of two ways :

i. ' Either by his own reasoning,'

ii. ' Or in so far as his intellect is enlightened by the divine power.'

When one reads this double process in prayer one asks oneself what is it but that which some call ' acquired ' and ' infused contemplation,' and which others prefer to call ' meditation ' and ' contemplation,' preferring to use the second word for the latter experience only ? In either case it is the realisation that is sought, not the mere learning more. Prayer is always a gift of God ; that is why St. Ignatius would have all prayer begin with a petition that He would teach us to pray. Sometimes in prayer the soul is left to work for itself, not to learn more, not even always to come to a conclusion, but to ' bring it home a little better,' to ' find more relish and spiritual fruit,' to ' fill and satisfy the soul.' Sometimes it will not need to work ; its ' intellect is enlightened by the divine power,' enabling it to ' feel and relish things internally.' Already, then, before a word of actual direction has been given, the director has been shown that ' infused contemplation,' as it is called, is the goal ; that his own words must, as far as possible, tend towards its awakening ; ' for it is not abundance of knowledge,' much less is it abundance of reasoning, ' that fills and satisfies the soul, but to feel and relish things interiorly.' More than once will he come back upon this distinction ; when realisation comes, let all the rest go. The mystics are the greatest of realists, because they go beneath the surface of life. They realise an existence more profound than that of this creation, they enjoy a satisfaction which no knowledge

of this world can give ; and it is precisely this
realisation, this 'interior sense and relish,' which St.
Ignatius, already in his second preliminary note, on
the first page of his book, lays down as the purpose
of all prayer, whether we call it 'contemplation' or
'meditation.' Perhaps, then, we need not wonder
why he seems to use the words indifferently.

In this Second Annotation we have another
characteristic word of the saint, the frequent use of
which confirms what has just been said. ' Interior,'
' interiorly,' and its variations are used by him in
the Exercises alone seventeen times ; they are
common in other places, especially in the Constitutions. In almost every case the word is used in a
peculiar way, which renders it untranslatable :
interior knowledge, interior sorrow, interior suffering, interior joy, etc. Nevertheless, though its
definition is not easy, it is a word which explains
itself. Perhaps the nearest equivalent in modern
English would be ' genuine,' the heart correspond-
ing to the external show ; it is akin to what St.
Paul repeatedly alludes to when he speaks of ' joy
in the heart,' ' charity unfeigned,' and the like. In
this the two saints are identical. Of all things else,
as seen in his book, in his letters, and in the sayings
recorded of him, St. Ignatius feared self-deception
in the spiritual life. He ' knew what was in man,'
and his tendency to deceive himself as well as
others by putting on a good appearance ; he knew
that men tended to judge one another by appearances, and to leave the inner reality alone. He had
come across false mystics, it would seem in abundance, he had suffered from unstable disciples ; the
ideal he had in mind needed more than outward

appearances for its foundation.  Hence it had
become with him almost a maxim, that every
exterior manifestation, whether of sanctity or of
anything else, if it did not come from within, if it
did not correspond exactly with the inner man, was
to be suspected.  It is this unbending adherence to
truth that has made him his enemies in all time.
In the following pages there will be so many
instances of this safeguarding of a man against
himself, in so many different directions, that it will
be enough here to point out its first application,
thus early, in regard to prayer.  Let a man be sincere in all things, the word seems to say, but above
all in regard to prayer.  There at least let the
exterior correspond with the interior ; let it not be
just knowledge, or skill, or philosophic understanding, and no more ; let it be in the heart, genuine,
and much else will inevitably follow.

Having thus secured the widest possible scope
for the understanding of prayer, St. Ignatius now
makes a frank acknowledgment.  In the ' Exercises,' as the name and the purpose imply, he is
about to use prayer mainly of a special kind and
for a definite end.  Still, this must not rule out any
other kind of prayer ;  on the contrary, the way he
fixes the limits within which he will use it shows
he knows of, and cherishes, and hopes for, something
more.  While the ' Exercises ' will be gone through
for one purpose, the general exercise will lead
beyond, to a greater knowledge and experience of
prayer.  Thus he tells us, in the Third Annotation :

' In all the following spiritual exercises [that
is, in all the " meditations or contemplations " to

be given in his book, for the special purpose he
has in view, but not necessarily in all prayer] we
use acts of the understanding when we reason,
and of the will for affective acts.'

Some may instantly conclude that by this explanation St. Ignatius would make all his meditations
what is miscalled ' discursive ' prayer, ruling out
what is further called ' pure ' contemplation.  But
this interpretation is scarcely consistent with what
has gone before.  Prayer is not truly prayer, in his
mind, so long as it is merely ' discursive ' ;  for ' it
is not abundance of knowledge that satisfies the
soul, but to feel and relish things interiorly ' ;  and
this is seen, again and again, in every one of the
' exercises ' that he has chosen to develop.  Moreover, the rest of this same Annotation, which is the
explicit reason for its being written, is a sufficient
disclaimer.  Reasoning, he has said, is the work of
the understanding, affections are the work of the
will ;  then at once :

> ' In the acts of the will, when we speak vocally
> or mentally with God Our Lord or with His
> saints, greater reverence is required on our part
> than when we are using the reason for under-
> standing.'

May we not say that here we catch the saint himself at prayer, unconsciously setting us an example
of how we ought to pray ?  He has chosen his subject for prayer ;  he has let his mind think about
it ;  while he has thought, his affections have been
aroused, against himself, in love of one or other of
those who have been brought before him, and have

been realised in all their beautiful truth, there, then, even as he prayed. Immediately all else has fallen away. He is in the presence of ' God Our Lord,' as he loves to call Him. He speaks with Him for he cannot help expressing his heart, sometimes breaking out in some ejaculation of words, sometimes with emotions in his heart which words cannot express, all the time his whole external demeanour showing the influence of that presence, the kneeling body, the reverence before his Lord, the face lit up with a light not of this earth. Only one whose habitual prayer has been of this kind could have written this Annotation, platitudinous as at first it may seem ; but the fact that he wrote it, and that he put it down so early among his notes, gives some hint of the heights to which he hoped to raise the soul that would follow his guidance. 'When we speak, mentally or vocally, with God Our Lord and His saints.' This was the ideal, and the reality ; this was what prayer was really to mean ; intercourse, personal and intimate, with reasoning deliberately set aside. For the soul has found whom it loveth ; it has held Him and will not let Him go.

When, then, we join this admonition with what St. Ignatius has said in the preceding Annotations, we are already able to form some idea of what he means by ' meditation or contemplation.' It is somewhat like this :

(1) The purpose, or the satisfaction, of prayer is to ' feel and relish things interiorly.' Later he will tell us many times that when this is attained we must put all else aside ; we must not ' reason ' any more, we must not seek to push on any further.

(2) This is attained, sometimes and in part, ' by one's own reasoning,' but much more when ' the intellect is enlightened by the divine power.' It is not for us to say when the latter shall come, for it is a pure gift of the divine bounty ; and so long as it does not come, even the greatest man of prayer must go on as best he can ' with reasoning of his own.'

(3) When this prayer of our own is employed ' we use acts of the understanding ' ; but even these, for true prayer, must always lead to ' acts of the will, when we speak, vocally or mentally, with God Our Lord or with His saints.'

(4) When these acts are reached, then, as the word itself implies, we pray in the true sense ; and then in consequence, being actually and consciously in the presence of ' God Our Lord, greater reverence is required.' Before, he had insisted on the interior, as making the exterior more genuine ; now he insists on the exterior, as a consequence and sign of that which is interior. If a man realises himself as standing in the presence of his ' Lord,' he will behave himself accordingly ; if his reflection on the fact makes no difference, then it is imaginative, speculative only and not real. If he observes due reverence his prayer will grow deeper ; if he is careless he will ordinarily find that God will be less intimate with him.

To this we may be allowed one reflection. Platitudinous, obvious as the Annotation may seem, perhaps the neglect of it alone explains the complaint of many who say they find prayer always dry. Perhaps they never come really into the presence of God at all ; they are too preoccupied with themselves, they wish to follow their own thoughts and reasoning, they do not look up to Him who alone can give light. Or perhaps, when the presence of God is real, they fail at the same time to realise the reverence that the conscious presence of God demands. Certainly that reverence points the way to that intimate knowledge of God which marks the lives of the mystics, and every deed they perform. Prayer and reverence go together.

Having defined the meaning of ' Spiritual Exercises ' in terms of self-conquest and prayer ; having safeguarded true ' contemplation ' against excess of intellectual reasoning ; having strengthened the soul of prayer by subjecting to it the behaviour of the body ; the saint next turns to the Exercises themselves. He asks how long they should last, and replies :

' The exercises should be completed in thirty days, or a little more or less.'

Clearly this cannot have been an arbitrary fixing of time ; it must have been the conclusion after long experience. But this does not concern us here ; more important is the mentality which this fourth Annotation reveals. He divides the Exercises into four ' weeks,' but warns us against taking the word literally, as a period of time. These four ' weeks ' are to correspond with

' the four parts with which the Exercises are divided ; that is to say, the first is the consideration and contemplation of sins ; the second is the life of Christ Our Lord until Palm Sunday ; the third, the Passion of Christ Our Lord ; the fourth, the Resurrection and Ascension, setting forth three methods of prayer.'

Here let us begin by noticing his description of the ' first ' part of the Exercises, and the use he makes of the word ' contemplation.' He speaks of ' the consideration and contemplation of sins.' Some will say at once that this only shows that St. Ignatius uses the words ' meditation ' and ' contemplation ' indifferently, looking on them as synonymous ; another writer would have written, ' the consideration of, and meditation on, sins.' To this it must be replied that if we give both the words the saint's own interpretation of them it is true ; but it is not true if we make the distinction between them that is made by many writers. Many mean by ' meditation ' what they call ' discursive prayer ' and nothing else ; by ' contemplation,' by contrast, they mean that kind of prayer which does not reason, and which begins with what is called the Prayer of Simplicity. They make a sharp distinction between the two, almost as if they were incompatible ; hence when one wishes to practise the first one must discard the other. Now St. Ignatius, along with St. Teresa and St. John of the Cross, would make no such absolute distinction. The difference is not one of essence, but of gradation or degree. St. Ignatius would have all prayer begin as it may, as the soul can at the given moment. Usually, that is, for most ordinary souls, this will be by stirring thought, the mind, ' raising it to God ' by use of the imagination, or by reasoning, or in any other way whatsoever. Experience has taught him, and the experience of every other soul he has met has confirmed it, that prayer cannot be made, with any fruit, at random as it were ; the more it is ordered and controlled at the beginning, and directed when direction is needed, the better it will be, ' the more solid,' to use the term employed by St. Teresa. But he is prepared, and he expects, to drop this finding of thoughts and reasons at any time ; and that no matter what may be the subject of prayer. There comes a moment when, ' either by his own reasoning, or in so far as his intellect is enlightened by the divine power,' the soul needs to ' reason ' no more ; it sees, it feels, it is moved, it realises, it utters itself in prayer ; and the sooner this comes the better. This is Contemplation, in his mind and in the mind of other contemplatives ; it is precisely by this process that St. Teresa and St. John of the Cross would have true contemplation to take root and grow.

Hence when St. Ignatius speaks of ' contemplation of sins,' he means exactly what he says ; he does not mean ' meditation ' in the former assumed sense. ' Meditation,' in that sense, there may have been ; but it is over and the soul now sees the horror of the thing, the foulness of the sin-stained soul, the unspeakable insult of it all in the sight of God. He means that the prayer of ' contemplation ' is as applicable to sin as to any other subject, to what offends God as well as to what pleases Him ; a truth of which we have abundant illustration in David, in St. Peter, St. Paul, and St. Augustine, in St. Teresa, St. Catherine of Genoa, St. John Vianney. And this is made the more clear from what follows in the same Annotation. There he speaks of the fruit of the First Week, ' what they seek,' what he has himself in mind when he treats of sin ; and this he defines, not as a General Confession and a firm purpose of amendment, some-

G

thing practical as some would say—these are not so much as mentioned—but as ' contrition, sorrow, tears for sins.'  He writes :

> ' Since it happens that in the first week some are slower in attaining what they seek, that is to say, contrition, sorrow, tears for their sins, and likewise since some may be more earnest than others, and more stirred or tempted by different spirits, it is sometimes requisite to contract the week, and at other times to lengthen it.'

This is to say, that the terminus of the First Week is no more nor less than a higher form of prayer than that which the soul had when it began. It is a truly contemplative state, as contrasted with one of reasoning and examination, perhaps even of acts.  The soul began with earnestness, with a determination to get clear of its sins once for all and to begin life anew ;  it may be that it had no other purpose in mind.  But it has learnt more than its own sins ;  it has grown in the knowledge and understanding of them, in the realisation of what they mean in the sight of God.  Probably it has already made its General Confession, and its purpose of amendment ; still, for the end he has in view, the saint is not satisfied with that.  Suddenly one day, for usually the grace comes on a sudden, the soul awakens to the truth.  It sees as in a vision the horror of sin in itself, the foulness of its own being by contact with it.  It is ashamed at the reality, till it longs to hide itself away ;  it is contrite, not in words only, but in its very heart ;  so real is its grief and regret that it can scarcely restrain its tears.  It looks about for relief ;  it is at the mercy of feelings, of spirits, of which, before, it had no conception. It is now in despair, now consoled ; now wondering whether it can ever be forgiven, now lost in loving confidence. The tears come to its eyes, and it cannot say whether they are of sorrow or of joy ; it does not clearly know whether it is the most miserable or the happiest of men. It has come into a new world ; it has not only resolved to begin its life anew, but life itself has now a new meaning ; it has become subject to those emotions, and disturbances, and trials, of which all mystical writers speak. When this occurs, says St. Ignatius in this Annotation, the soul is in the ' state ' required for further development and must push on. St. John of the Cross would say it has completed its ' Ascent of Mount Carmel ' ; it has experienced the first horror of the ' Dark Night of the Soul.'

From this it is clear that when St. Ignatius put down his ' meditations ' on sin and its concomitants, he had in mind ' contemplation,' and the making of the contemplative, not merely the purification of the sinner. On this account he would give his Exercises to only one person at a time ; Faber, Xavier, Borgia, and the rest, all were taken one by one, and the result in every case was an ecstatic contemplative. But this was only the beginning, the necessary consequence, as St. Thomas Aquinas and his disciples would say, of the soul genuinely doing what it could. There would be much more to come, for the soul that God would raise to higher things ; much that would make the bravest heart quail. No one issues this warning more than St. John of the Cross ; he describes its degrees, at least in its first stages, perhaps less by what it

contains than by the sacrifices and trials it will cost.
So is it with the author of the Exercises. He has
sufficiently explained his definitions ; he now turns
to the exercitant himself. If the First Week will
cost him much, what comes after may cost more ;
if his client is to become the man he would have him
become, in word or in deed, in action or in contemplation, it matters not which so the will of God
is done, he must be prepared for great sacrifices.
Here, then, he thinks it worth while to write :

> ' He who receives the Exercises will benefit
> much by entering upon them with great courage
> and generosity towards his Creator and Lord,
> offering to Him all his will and freedom, in order
> that His Divine Majesty may make use alike of
> his person, and of all that he has, according to
> His most holy Will.'

The wording of this encouragement compels us
to anticipate. It will recur again and again, in
various forms, during all the Exercises ; at the end,
when we look at the last prayer of all, the Colloquy
for the ' Contemplation for Obtaining Love,' we
find almost exactly the same words. There, as the
crowning offering of all when the thirty days are
over, the exercitant, it is assumed, will say ' with
much affection ' :

> ' Take, Lord, and receive all my liberty, my
> memory, my understanding, and all my will, all
> that I have and possess : you gave it me, to you,
> Lord, I return it : all is yours, dispose of it
> according to all your will : give me your love
> and your grace, which is enough for me.'

Naturally we ask ourselves what is the difference between this closing prayer of all the Exercises, and the prayer recommended at the beginning ; for certainly they contain the same offering, and the same purpose. The answer is contained in all that has been done during those thirty days ; after they are over that same prayer has so come to be ' felt and relished interiorly ' that it has become another thing. In the Annotation at the beginning the exercitant has been encouraged to make it ' with great courage and generosity towards his Creator and Lord ' ; at the end it is made ' with gratitude,' and ' with much affection.' The words are indeed the same, but contemplation with love has opened the soul's eyes ; so that what at first needed ' great courage and generosity ' now becomes spontaneous and easy, the prompting, irresistible, of purest love. It is not, then, by accident that the language is the same ; the saint has kept the one formula, and has let its meaning grow, as he has explained in his second Annotation. Neither at the beginning nor at the end is there any word of action, beyond that of complete surrender ; even, if need be, to utter inaction, since memory, understanding, will, and all else are put away. In both it is the contemplative plane that is visualised, as the contemplative himself well knows. It contains almost the definition of the state of contemplation, that state which has so little use for what ' the world loves and embraces.'

# III

## THE PLACE OF SPIRITUAL DIRECTION : THE DIRECTOR AND THE EXERCITANT

HAVING thus, more or less—for there is much yet to learn, but that can only come from practice and experience—laid down the importance of prayer, its meaning, its process, its object, its stages, St. Ignatius now turns to him who gives the Exercises. And first, as if to emphasise what has gone before, he shows him he must make the prayer of the exercitant the barometer by which he may estimate the atmosphere of the retreat. If the exercitant is merely reasoning and drawing conclusions, however good and sound they may be, there is something wrong ; the result is the fruit of study only, it is philosophy and no more, and though even that may give a man a new outlook on life it is not the stirring of the heart, the awakening of a new life, which St. Ignatius seeks. For the man who prays, who ' feels and relishes things interiorly ' and does not merely think, there should be something more ; if he ' experiences no spiritual motions,' if he has no special ' consolations or desolations,' if he ' is not moved by different spirits,' then his prayer must be somewhere at fault. The saint considers nothing else ; if the prayer is wrong, and is unproductive, not in resolutions but in the prayer itself, then the retreat is not going as it should, and the director should look to it. There is almost a note of anxiety in what he now writes ; not about conclusions or resolutions, which are left entirely to look after themselves, but about the prayer, and it alone. He writes as his first admonition :

'When he who gives the exercises perceives that the exercitant experiences no spiritual motions in his soul, such as consolations or desolations, and is not moved by different spirits, he should question him narrowly about the exercises, whether he makes them at the times fixed, and in what manner, and also about the additions, whether he diligently practises them, questioning him particularly in each of these matters.'

The director is then referred to two places in the Exercises, in one of which rules are given ' for the Discernment of Spirits,' in the other certain hints for the better management of prayer. If the first Annotations, hitherto considered, show the paramount, almost absolute, importance St. Ignatius attaches to prayer, the Rules for the Discernment of Spirits show us better than anything else the experiences he looks for in prayer. And that at the very beginning ; the first set of rules, and therefore the states of soul they describe, are expressly said to be more fitting to the First Week, that is, the earliest stage, when the soul is still engaged with its own purification. Since it is assumed that the giver of the Exercises takes these Rules as his standard, below which he will not go, it may be well to discuss them here ; those at least which refer to the first stages.

These Rules are so described :

> ' Rules in order to feel and understand in some manner the various motions that are produced in the soul : the good ones that they may be accepted, and the evil that they may be cast out : and they are more suitable for the First Week.'

The last sentence of this quasi-definition expressly says that the Rules are specially suitable for souls still in the Purgative Way, who are not yet understood to have advanced far in prayer, who are chiefly engaged in the preliminary work of clearing the ground, producing, so far as they may, the cleanness of heart which shall see God. Now St. Ignatius, like other genuine mystical writers as contrasted with mystical students, has a way of saying what, at first sight, seems an obvious platitude, and yet what, when considered, is found to contain some deep reflection on life. Such is the case with these Rules. A first reading may see nothing in them ; yet a volume could be written to show how they are the fruit of experience of men, when they are face to face with the supernatural. The First Rule, for example, reads :

> ' In persons who go from mortal sin to mortal sin, the enemy is commonly accustomed to suggest to them apparent pleasures, making them imagine sensual delights and pleasures, the more to preserve and increase them in their vices and sins. With such persons the good spirit uses a contrary method, stinging them and causing their consciences remorse by the dictate of the reason.'

In this first Rule are laid down two principles, obviously true enough, the fruit of common sense and common experience, yet, in practice, lending themselves to abuse and contradiction at every turn. When a man is going from bad to worse his conscience tells him what he is doing ; that in the end he will bring about his own ruin, and his reason knows it. Still another part of him says that it does not care ; it will not be dictated to, it will have its own way ; it claims the right to enjoy itself, to satisfy itself, and the evil it contemplates promises that satisfaction. Let ruin come or not, it will be its own master. Thus is the constant struggle in the degenerating soul, till, at last, conscience and reason are stifled ; finally conquered reason is forced to the will that has conquered it, and it finds arguments to make evil appear as good, wrong as right. It is a familiar process, going on about us every day, not only in individuals, but also in public opinion and life. When a state finds reasons to sanction as good what nature knows to be evil, what former generations have shrunk from as intrinsically bad, then we have an infallible sign that it is on the downward grade, from unhappiness to unhappiness whatever the appearance, from true security to false, whatever may show on the surface.

On the other hand, when a man is really anxious to live a better life, to have done with evil and be true to himself, the process is reversed. Conscience, which before annoyed, now encourages him ; reason, which before distressed, now helps him ; at every bold step taken he experiences a satisfaction, a joy, a determination to go yet further forward, which he has not felt before. But at the

same time there is another part of him which makes
him hesitate.  It tells him that the step he is about
to take is too much for him ;  he has sunk too low,
and cannot hope so easily to recover.  The cost is
too great ;  he cannot now forgo the pleasures
which have become part of his life ;  he will succeed
better at another time, under other conditions,
when circumstances are more suitable.  This is the
meaning of the Second Rule :

> ' In the persons who are proceeding earnestly,
> purging their sins and rising from well to better
> in the service of God Our Lord, the method is
> the contrary to that in the first rule.  For then
> it is peculiar to the evil spirit to cause remorse,
> to sadden, and to place impediments, disquieting
> with false reasons in order that they may not
> advance ;  and it is peculiar to the good spirit to
> give courage and strength, consolations, tears,
> inspirations and quiet, making things easy, and
> getting rid of all impediments, in order that they
> may advance further in the good work.'

How much might be written to show the truth
of the principles given in these two Rules, both in
the individual and in public life.  Evil encourages
evil, and finds specious justifications to call it good ;
evil opposes good, and invariably finds pretexts to
put it in the wrong.  When evil proves another to
be wicked we may be almost sure that the other is
good and right.  But the action of evil, and of him
who ' goes from bad to worse,' does not concern
us here.  The eyes of the writer are on the other
type ;  on the man who is in earnest, who wishes
to be clean in the sight of God, and to take up his

duty 'with great courage and generosity towards
His Creator and Lord.'  Such a man, we know full
well, God will not leave deserted ; ' facienti quod
in se est, Deus non denegat gratiam.'  Then every
effort to do his best will stir new emotions.  God
will take those emotions and will strengthen them,
even while He leaves the soul to win its own victory,
and so earn its own reward.  He will inspire them
with hope when they promised only failure, He
will surround them with peace when all was storm,
He will draw the soul on till it finds, in union with
Him, its recompense exceeding great.  Still, to St.
Ignatius, such a soul is only at the beginning of
its course, and beginners, from mere inexperience,
are liable to miss their way.  When they are filled
with this new joy of the Lord they may mistake it
for conquest secured ;  when it fades, for it is
certain that it will fade, they may mistake it for
defeat.  ' In my abundance I said : I shall never
be moved. . . . Thou turnedst away thy face from
me and I became troubled.'  Such beginners,
inexperienced in the discernment of spirits, must be
shown clearly the significance of both the one and
the other, of both solid and fleeting joy, of passing
and permanent trouble ;  and St. Ignatius proceeds,
be it noticed thus early, while he deals with souls as
yet only in the Purgative Way, to give definitions
of ' Consolation ' and ' Desolation ' which might
well have come from St. John of the Cross, or St.
Teresa, or any of the greatest mystics.  Thus, in
the Third Rule, he speaks of ' spiritual consolation ':

' I call it " consolation " when there is caused
in the soul some interior motion with which the

soul comes to be inflamed in love of its Creator
and Lord ;  and consequently, when it cannot
love any created thing on the face of the earth
in itself, but only in the Creator of them all.
Likewise when it sheds tears inciting to love of
its Lord :  now, it may be, out of sorrow for its
sins, or at the Passion of Christ Our Lord, or for
other things expressly directed to His service and
praise.  Finally, I call " consolation " all increase
of hope, faith, and charity, and all interior joy
which calls and draws to heavenly things and to
the salvation of one's own soul, quieting it and
pacifying it in its Creator and Lord.'

This definition is immediately followed by that
of ' spiritual desolation ' :

' I call " desolation " everything contrary to
the above rule ;  such as darkness of the soul,
trouble within it, motion to base and earthly
things, disquiet from various agitations and temptations, a moving to misgivings, without hope,
without love, finding itself altogether slothful,
tepid, sad, and as though separated from its
Creator and Lord.  For just as consolation is
contrary to desolation, in the same way the
thoughts which spring from consolation are contrary to the thoughts which spring from desolation.'

As we quote these two definitions the pen, almost
of itself, would run on with countless parallel passages from all the mystics, but especially from St.
John of the Cross.  We ask whether there is, in all
spiritual literature, a more perfect compendium of

the teaching of the mystical doctor, as it is elaborated in *The Spiritual Canticle* and *The Dark Night of the Soul*. It is mystic from beginning to end. The exercitant is tested, not by the completeness of his confession, not by his purpose of amendment, not by any resolutions he may have fixed upon ; none of these are so much as mentioned. He is tested simply by the progress he has made in prayer and mystical experience ; the keenness of his love, and that of a kind he has never before thought possible ; the tears he has shed, of which, before, he might even have been ashamed ; the realisation of hope, and faith, and charity, making his soul crave for the joy that is not of this world ; or else that darkness and unrest, almost that sense of nausea which has made him feel for a time like a soul in despair or possessed. And this while yet he is in no more than the first stage, ' the First Week,' as the title of the ' Rules ' expressly says : while yet he has got no further than ' meditating or contemplating ' sin and all its effects. Has the vivid truth come home to him so that he does not need to ' think ' about it any more ? Has he seen himself as he really is, with all his meanness and malice ? Has he seen the hand of an offended God held back, by a Father's love, by a Brother's blood, and himself thus saved from what justice might have demanded ? Has the realisation carried him beyond himself, to the feet of the Father who has been contemned, and yet out of love has forgiven ? Has this led him even to tears, so real has the truth become ; tears of sorrow, tears of love, tears of regret, tears of joy, he scarcely knows himself what to call them ? Has he thus been suddenly lifted up, from despair to hopeful assurance, from doubt to faith that is knowledge, from humiliating self-contempt to boundless love, from the misery of guilt to unspeakable joy, from the restlessness of the sinner to the peace and quiet of the sonship of God?

Or has it been the other way? Has the light come on a sudden, and then, as suddenly, gone out? Has it been that the exercitant who, at ordinary times, could make his confession and act of contrition quite regularly, now has found that he does not seem to be able to do so much as that? He began in deadly earnest; he did as he was recommended, renewing his courage and generosity; he sincerely desired to give to God all he could. But it has all gone contrary to his expectation. Seldom if ever before has he been so interiorly worried or tried with the knowledge of himself, and he can give himself no explanation. When he entered the retreat he determined to put everything else aside; yet he has been tried with idle dreams and speculations, of old grievances, of future plans, of anxieties concerning the present, far more than they could have troubled him had he been going through his usual routine. More and worse than all this, he has been vilely tempted in a way to make him uneasy. Old fascinations have risen up that he thought long dead, new possibilities of sin have been pictured in his mind, making him wonder whether he can be really forgiven, or whether he can be in earnest after all. And there has seemed to be no escape. He has averted his mind but the visions have returned; he has tried to pray against it all and there has been no relief. He has been tempted to grow weary of the struggle ; to tell himself that this new life is not for him ; to wonder whether, after all, what he has been assured can be true, whether there is not a limit to the patience of God and he has passed it ; he is tempted to blank despair.

These are the two ' states ' which St. Ignatius anticipates in the very first days of the Exercises, and he bids the director to be ready for them. When he discovers the second, let him not be alarmed ; to be so troubled is a good sign, the bad sign would be if the exercitant had no experiences or emotion: at all. Let him deal gently with such a case ; let him be kind and encouraging. Let him point out how all this is only what might be expected ; for the enemy is not likely to submit to a conquest of a soul without some kind of struggle. It will pass, the dawn will come ; in the meantime let him go on, changing nothing of his good resolutions, changing only that which may seem likely to remove the cloud that overshadows him. He is tempted to pray less ; perhaps, then, a little more prayer will make all the difference. He shuns self-examination ; perhaps this is only a subtle form of dishonesty with himself, and a little more vigour will put it right. He is not afraid of, but is merely disgusted with, penance ; perhaps not so much for the sake of the penance itself, but in order to secure self-mastery, a little extra penance will do him no harm. In any case let him not lose heart. God puts him through this trial only that he may know himself the better, and that he may become yet more zealous after cleanness of heart. Now he realises how helpless he is of himself, how of himself he can do nothing. But the grace of God is with him, however little, for the moment, he may recognise it. The fervour he had before is not lessened, it is only less felt; love still grows in his heart and will be the stronger from this very trial; grace still abounds, and God is faithful. The desolation will not last, consolation will follow it, and when it comes it will be greater and deeper, on more solid foundation than ever it had been before.

At this point we are given another illustration of the agreement of St. Ignatius with the traditional teaching of theologians and mystics. He has just spoken as though consolation, or progress in prayer, depended on the soul's own efforts :

'Let him who is in desolation consider how the Lord has left him, as a probation, to his natural powers, in order that he may resist the various agitations and temptations of the enemy ; for he can do so with the divine help, which always remains to him, though he does not feel it clearly, because the Lord has taken away from him his much fervour, ever-growing love and intense grace ; yet grace sufficient for eternal salvation remains to him.'

This is the language of St. Thomas and the scholastics ; let the soul do what it can, and infallibly God will do the rest. Still the soul must not forget that ' the rest,' elevation in prayer of any kind, depends ultimately not on itself. Of itself it can hinder prayer ; if in spite of effort desolation still remains, it is but that, for some good reason, God withholds His hand. The next Rule is full of significance. It is written by one who looks for ' spiritual consolations ' in the soul, even at this early stage ; but who would have them well grounded on humility and truth. He writes :

'There are three principal reasons why we find ourselves desolate. The first is on account of being tepid, slothful or negligent in our spiritual exercises, and therefore on account of our faults spiritual consolation abandons us. The second, in order to prove what we are worth, and how we progress in His service and praise without such salary of consolations and ever-growing graces. The third, to give us true knowledge and understanding in order that we may feel intimately that it is not in our power to bring in or keep ever-growing devotion, intense love, tears, or any other spiritual consolation, but that all is the gift and grace of God Our Lord.'

'Devotion, love, tears, spiritual consolation'; these are the fruits of prayer put before the soul when it is still in its ' week ' of purgation, ' contemplating ' sin and its effects. Reasoning, the saint says in effect, will never bring it to these ; only God can, and will. It will be tossed to and fro ; there will be consolation, there will be desolation, and the soul needs to be kept evenly balanced. When it enjoys consolation, when it has ' devotion, love, tears,' let it enjoy them to the full ; but let it not forget that they will not always be the same, that they are no proof of the soul's own strength. But neither is desolation a proof of weakness :

'Let him who is consoled endeavour to humble and abase himself as much as he can, thinking how little he can do in the time of desolation

H

without such grace or consolation.  On the contrary, let him who is in desolation think that with the sufficient grace he can do much to resist his enemies, taking strength in his Creator and Lord.'

When we read all this, set before the director of the Exercises as the one fundamental matter for his attention, we are almost tempted to ask whether St. Ignatius has forgotten the purpose with which he began.  He set out to train a man to seek, find, and fulfil the will of God.  Already he seems to have set this aside, and to be intent on training a man of prayer ;  and not only that, but he assumes, even from the first, that such a man, if he is faithful, will have subtle experiences in his soul.  And yet not all ;  the saint is too experienced in the ways of human nature to think that every soul can be a mystic, indeed, for many, treating of such things is a danger.  This is the meaning of the ninth Annotation :

> ' It should be noticed that when the exercitant is engaged in the exercises of the first week, if he be a person inexperienced in spiritual matters, and if he be grossly and openly tempted, as by alleging difficulties to his advance in the service of God Our Lord, such as labours, shame, and fear of losing worldly honour, etc. ;  let not him who gives the exercises speak to him of the rules about the different spirits belonging to the second week, for they will injure him as much as the rules of spirit for the first week will benefit him, the matter contained being too subtle and too sublime for him to be able to understand.'

Thus St. Ignatius suggests that distinction between souls, which is confirmed by the experience of everyone who has had to deal with them, however much, in theory, it may be true that all souls are alike called to the highest states of prayer. In matter of fact very few arrive there, and most of the rest fail through no fault of their own. There are two classes of souls, and they may be distinguished by two classes of temptations ; classes not so distinct that a soul may not pass from one class to the other, nor necessarily holier, one than the other, but simply as a matter of experience. There are those who, however good in themselves they may be, yet, whether from circumstances or from temperament, know little of the spiritual life. They are, perhaps, compelled to be engrossed in the affairs of this life and can scarcely avoid estimating values accordingly. They are tempted, as St. Ignatius calls it, ' grossly and openly,' that is by measurements as this world sees them. They may say that too great advance in God's service costs too much, that it unfits them for the part they must play among other men, that it puts an end to success and promotion in this world, and so on. The saint, either here or elsewhere, does not speak in condemnation of such people ; on the contrary later on he caters specially for them. He merely says, and it is a warning of importance but easily neglected, that to souls of that mentality it is useless, nay, it is ' injurious,' to speak of prayer, and the movements of the soul in prayer, on any but the ordinary plane. Such souls will not gain, but will suffer, from reading such authors as St. Teresa or St. John

of the Cross.  For the time being at least let
them be content with the ordinary things of the
spiritual life, even in time of retreat.  One day, it
may be, their eyes will be opened and they will
see, ' contemplate ' as in a new vision, themselves
and their sins, and will break down, spontaneously
and completely, in ' contrition, sorrow, tears.'
When that day comes they may be taken further ;
but before that day, to study the rules of the
mystical life, even of the second or ' Illuminative '
degree, can do them little good and may even be
injurious.

But there are others who are capable of going
much further, and the experienced director will
not be slow to recognise them.  Instead of being
' grossly and openly tempted, as by alleging difficulties, etc.,' they will be ' assailed and tempted
under the appearance of good.'  They will see no
difficulty anywhere that need be feared ;  they will
make even difficulties a reason for going forward
with a bound.  They will see only joy and satisfaction in the service of the Lord ;  having rid
themselves of their burthen they will be filled with
' good and holy thoughts ' ;  they will ignore
whither they may lead, telling themselves that what
is good and holy can only end in what is holy and
good.  They will tend to be imprudent, to mortify
themselves more than is wise, to undertake tasks
that are beyond them, to give themselves up to
prayer which the soul in its present state cannot
sustain, and which in time, when the fervour has
abated, either will weary and flag or else will
become dull quietism, or exalted pride, or both.
This is the new state of one who makes progress

in prayer.   It is the dawning of the Illuminative
Way, and

> ' the enemy of human nature usually tempts
> more under the semblance of good when a
> person is exercising himself in the illuminative
> life.'

How he tempts him is elsewhere described :

> ' It is peculiar to the bad angel, who " trans-
> forms himself into an angel of light," to enter
> with the devout soul and take his own way out ;
> that is to say, to bring good and holy thoughts
> suitable to such a just soul, and afterwards, little
> by little, he tries to get his own way, bringing the
> soul into his hidden wiles and perverse intentions.'

The far-reaching significance of this shrewd comment anyone can see ;  but it is, essentially, the
comment of a contemplative, who has gone far in
the way of prayer.   In the former place he has
thrown action aside, treating it only as a source of
' gross and open ' temptation ;  now he is dealing
with a soul that is free, and his one purpose is to
enable it to go forward untrammelled.   But there
is the other danger, even greater than the former,
which every contemplative has experienced, both
in himself and in others.   Most heresies have begun
from the teaching of something good : Pelagianism,
Lutheranism, Molinism, Modernism have all set
out from ' good and holy thoughts.'   So is it with
Communism, or with any of the modern ideals ;
it is precisely because they can be shown to be
' good and holy ' in their outlook and purpose that
all the evil that is done in their name, the work of

'the enemy of human nature,' can be ignored. And if this is true so far afield, much more is it true on the purely spiritual plane. The fantastic heresies of the earliest centuries, the Flagellants and other vagaries in the Middle Ages, the Puritans in our own country, with their concomitants else-where, were all 'good and holy' in their origin and motive ; 'little by little' the 'enemy of human nature' was able to draw them 'into his hidden wiles and perverse intentions.' Worst of all, and with this St. Ignatius is specially concerned, the same may happen in the realm of prayer. Illu-minism, which was rife in his time, Quietism, which followed soon after, the Jansenism of Port Royal, all found their beginnings in that which was 'good and holy' ; even to this day all have their adherents in 'good and holy' souls. But Illuminism led to moral corruption, Quietism led to contempt of law, Port Royal led to hard pride ; all three, in the name of all that is 'good and holy,' have given 'the enemy of human nature . . . his own way.'

It is important to emphasise this obvious truth, for it is so obvious that it may be easily passed over as a platitude. But St. Ignatius would not have it passed over ; to him that period of tran-sition, when the soul of prayer passes from its time of cleansing into the new light, is the most crucial moment of all its career. If at this step it goes aright, all is likely to be well in the future ; the day will come when it will rise to higher heights in prayer, when it will be absorbed in love. But, naturally, since it is the crucial moment, 'the enemy of our human nature' will be particularly active. He will offer the soul forbidden fruit; he will tell it that the eating of it will bring it to the knowledge of good and evil, will make it like to God; he will assure it that it will not die the death. It has seen the beauty of prayer; let it give itself up to the same, under the guidance of the angel of light. Let it lay aside all trammels and encumbrances in the way to God, and lose itself in the embrace of His love. Let it leap forward at once to the contemplation of the Beatific Vision, ignoring the petty images and fancies of the human brain that only impede and obscure the sight. Let it stand for itself, alone in the divine Presence; let it pass over the warnings of saints who have known no better than the hard road, and have written for their like. Or if it listens to them, let it select those places which are intended for chosen souls like itself. Let it leave the rest to others, who can pray only with a book, who need the Gospels to help them, who can get no further than the humanity of Christ, who, when they pray to God, must needs do so by means of acts of faith, hope, and charity. Let it leave all this behind, neglect it as inferior; let it follow ' the angel of light ' who now guides it, and rise above the cumbersome things of the flesh. The soul may listen, and pray accordingly; and soon, if it is not awakened, may ' thank God that it is not as the rest of men.' St. Ignatius has watched the process of corruption, common enough among the people around him. He has felt its beginnings in himself, and he knows that by no other way can growth in prayer be more efficiently checked. Even if it does not lead to pride, it paralyses; the soul discovers that it can go no further, but must veer about till at last it grows weary. Therefore at this point he has given his warning and his rules of caution, not that he may hinder contemplative prayer but that he may secure it ; that he may give the contemplative himself safe guidance in this most difficult of journeys, which ' the enemy of human nature, transformed into an angel of light,' will assure him is so easy.

IV

# THE SECOND STAGE OF DIRECTION

WE have seen how from the beginning St. Ignatius would have prayer alone, and experiences in prayer, the barometer to mark the atmosphere of the soul while it goes through the Spiritual Exercises. If there are no emotions, perhaps we would now call them reactions, no temptations on the one hand and no illuminations, realisations, on the other, he doubts whether all can be going as it ought ; if all is well, if the exercitant is striving with ' large heart and generosity,' there must come ' consolations ' or ' desolations,' loving experiences of the presence and love of God, or the sense of abandonment because He seems far away. He appears to be concerned about nothing else ; confession, purpose of amendment are not so much as mentioned ; even resolutions are looked at with caution, and in some cases the exercitant is told to put them aside. His one care is that the penitent shall pray well, so well that he shall experience, and grow in the experience of, the deeper things of prayer, shall not have that growth interrupted or dwarfed, either by ignorance or by taking a wrong path. He has given the guidance needed for the beginner, yet it assumes very much : not to make of too great account the new delights he has discovered, not to be too discouraged when the light fades and the old temptations return.  Instead let him go forward steadfastly in prayer, striving all the more, the more he is tempted to relent, lengthening his prayer rather than shortening it, but praying, praying, at all costs.

This is the author's main matter of attention during the First Week, the week of purgation and study of sin.  He does not mind about confession ; he even hints in one place that the director should not also be the confessor, so that he may attend more to ' the various movements and thoughts to which the different spirits draw ' the exercitant. One day, to some sooner, to others later, the change will come.  They will no longer be tempted grossly, they will be tempted by false goodness. Thus the change is described :

> ' When he who is giving the exercises per- ceives that he who is receiving them is assailed and tempted under an appearance of good, then is the proper time to speak to him of the rules of the second week.  For the enemy of human nature usually tempts more under the semblance of good when a person is exercising himself in the illuminative life, which corresponds to the exer- cises of the second week ;  but not so much in the purgative life, which corresponds to the exercises of the first week.'

When this time comes, when the director has discovered that the penitent substitutes desire to do something for love and not only to sorrow, then he is ordered to alter, almost reverse, his tone.  A new set of Rules for Discernment of Spirits is given to him, quite different from the first ; indeed so different that St. Ignatius considers their application before the proper time to be even dangerous :

'For they will injure him [the exercitant still in the First Week] as much as the rules of spirits for the first week will benefit him, the matter contained being too subtle and too sublime for him to be able to understand.'

These Rules are thus defined :

'Rules to the same effect [i.e. to feel and understand in some manner the various motions that are produced in the soul : the good ones that they may be accepted, and the evil that they may be cast out] with greater discernment of spirits ; and they are more suitable for the Second Week.'

Obviously, for the guidance of the soul, St. Ignatius looks upon this second set of Rules as, perhaps, the most important chapter in the Exercises. Moreover, he has written them in such a way as to compel the reader to study them in contrast with the Rules he has given before. And yet, at first, they might seem to differ in nothing ; in fact, they differ only in the emphasis put on certain words. That is why he has said that their ' matter is too subtle and too sublime ' for the uninitiated to understand. Before, he had begun with a description of a soul who ' goes from mortal sin to mortal sin,' the allurements of false pleasures with which such a soul is tempted, and prick of conscience with which it is disturbed. He had gone on to show how with one who is ' proceeding earnestly . . ., rising from well to better in the service of God,' the opposite is the case ; for such a soul it is the devil who disturbs, whereas

> ' It is peculiar to the good spirit to give courage and strength, consolations, tears, inspirations and quiet, making things easy and getting rid of all impediments, in order that they may advance further in the good work.'

Now, in these Second Rules, the saint can discard the first case, the man who ' proceeds from mortal sin to mortal sin ' ; he need only consider him who is ' rising from well to better,' and indeed has already had experience of ' consolations, tears, inspirations, and quiet.' He has got himself free from his burthen, he has lifted up his eyes and seen ; for him, then, the former principle is resumed, but the emphasis is now reversed :

> ' It is peculiar to God and His angels in their motions to give true happiness and spiritual joy, removing all sadness and disturbance, which the enemy induces ; to the latter it is peculiar to fight against such joy and spiritual consolation, bringing apparent reason, subtleties, and persistent fallacies.'

We have already been told of the difference between false joy and true, between the pleasure of the persistent sinner and the joy in the heart of the man who is in earnest. We have had given to us the definition of ' consolation ' and ' desolation,' as the words are understood in spiritual experience. We have had Rules given to us for the better guid-

ance of the soul in desolation ; that it should learn
to stand firm :

> ' For just as in consolation it is rather the
> good spirit that guides and counsels us, so in
> desolation it is rather the evil one, with whose
> counsels we cannot take the way to do right.'

On the other hand, the soul in consolation has
been warned rather than encouraged. He has
been told that such consolation as he has so far
enjoyed is not likely to last ; that he must be prepared for reactions ; that the devil is not likely to
leave him so easily alone. Now the perspective is
altered ; we are not given warnings with encouragements, but rather encouragements with warnings ;
' happiness and spiritual joy ' are set before us in
all their attraction, so that, when the heart is
expanded, we may run the faster in the way of His
commandments.

With this introduction St. Ignatius now lays
down his absolute rule of Infused Contemplation.
No teacher of Mystical Theology has stated it more
clearly or more inclusively ; no one has set it more
in the forefront of his aim and ideal. The Second
Rule reads :

> ' It belongs solely to God Our Lord to give
> consolation to the soul without preceding cause ;
> for it is peculiar to the Creator to enter it, leave
> it, and cause motion in it, drawing it wholly to
> love of His Divine Majesty. I say without cause,
> without any previous feeling or knowledge of
> any object by which such consolation could come
> by means of acts of understanding and will.'

How exactly this expresses the mind of St. Teresa and St. John of the Cross after him, and of Dionysius and St. Augustine before him, when these saints speak of the deepest impressions of God upon the soul ! Human beings, as human beings, must think if they would grow in knowledge ; if they would grow in love, and action as the proof of love, they must use the will. So is it in prayer ; if they would advance in prayer, so long as they are human, they must themselves ' raise the mind and heart to God,' and thence gain their reward, their greater knowledge and love and joy in the Lord their God. But one day, whether while they are so striving, or whether they are at rest, or even sometimes in the midst of work, suddenly, for no reason that they know, without anything to cause it, they see what they have never seen before, they are conscious of a presence more intimate than they have ever known it, they would almost call it physical whereas before it was only intellectual, they experience a joy, a consolation, with which no other consolation they have hitherto had can compare. It is like a new creation, a new order of being ; it is as if one stood on solid ground even in the spiritual sphere ; it is a very breathing and a life of love, so deep that at last one is conscious that love goes beyond knowledge, one loves more than one knows. In how many ways the saints have tried to describe this state, dividing it and subdividing it that we may the better understand them, yet always leaving us, as it were, mystified, in a cloud, groping our way as best we may. St. Ignatius here describes the same, in few words, yet unmistakably ; and, let it be clearly noticed, he

sets down his Rule for those who are only beginning
the Illuminative Way.   Nor does he, as at the
beginning, make any exceptions.   For those who
go by that way, this goal will, without any doubt,
one day be theirs.

Having said this, clearly and without possibility
of doubt, the saint assumes that on that special
point he has said enough.   Once the soul is in the
hands and under the guidance of its loving Creator
and Lord he may leave it there ;  the work of the
director is then ended, and he need say no more.
This has already been emphasised in the Annotations ;  there the director has been told quite clearly
that his work is to bring the soul and its Creator
together ;  when that is done his task is over and
he must not interfere.   In a beautiful way he has
already said :

' He who gives the exercises should not move
him who receives them more to poverty and the
promise thereof than to their contraries, or more
to one state or manner of life than to another.
For although, outside the exercises, we may law-
fully and meritoriously move all persons who are
probably suited for it to choose continence, vir-
ginity, the religious state, and every kind of
evangelical perfection ;  yet during such spiritual
exercises it is more fitting and far better, in the
seeking of the divine will, that the Creator and
Lord Himself communicate Himself to His
devout soul, winning it to love and praise Him,
and disposing it for that way of life wherein it
will be better able to serve Him in the future.
Accordingly let not him who gives them lean or

incline himself to the one side or the other, but remain in the middle like a balance, and leave the Creator to act directly with the creature, and the creature with his Creator and Lord.'

This, then, is the ideal at which the Exercises aim. They would take a soul of whatever kind ; they would purify it, and that by means of prayer. They would then instruct it and practise it in prayer, from the most elementary conception of the term, until one day it sees, and knows, and is in direct communication with its Creator and Lord. When they have done that their chief work is done ; the rest will be between Creator and creature, creature and Creator, with no one and nothing coming between. Signs that this point has been reached will be the new experiences which the soul will receive. It will have consolations, joys, and even sorrows, certainties and yet further mysteries, for which it cannot account, which have been stirred by no effort or reasoning of its own. It will be conscious of the presence of God in a peculiar way, when He leaves it again it will have a sense of emptiness akin to death ; both alike will make it love and long for God all the more. It will want to be pleasing in His sight, just to please Him and nothing else. It will want to live the life He would have it live, just because He would so have it, and for no other reason. This is the ideal aimed at, expressed here in the Second Rule for Discernment of Spirits ; we do not know whether any contemplative has expressed his vocation more clearly.

But for the majority of men, indeed for all, not

excluding the sublimest of contemplatives, this direct and intimate union is not universal. Not everyone receives his spiritual consolations directly from the hand of God ; no one receives them thus always. Besides the consolation that comes straight from Him, there are others, far more common, which in some degree depend on ourselves ; we pray as best we can, we use the faculties of our soul to lift ourselves to God, and God through His angel rewards us by meeting us half-way. Such consolations, such heights of contemplative prayer may be true, but also they may have their false counterfeits ; and it is now that the soul that would defend itself against false mysticism must be put on its guard. This is the significance of the Rules now to follow. No one had endured greater false mystic temptations than their author ; his days in the cave at Manresa had been full of them. Therefore he wrote as one who had been through the experience and knew ; and, manifestly, he wrote, not to deter the soul from the higher things of contemplation but to make sure that it progressed towards them, and was not turned aside by will-o'-the-wisps.

He begins by a simple statement of the fact. He writes in the Third Rule :

' With a reason [i.e. founded on some natural cause, in contrast with those consolations of which he has already spoken], not only the good angel, but also the bad angel can console the soul, for their contrary ends ; the good angel for the profit of the soul, that it may grow and rise from good to better ; and the bad angel for the contrary, and that he may bring it eventually to his wicked intention and malice.'

I

The saint here states a fact which is illustrated again and again in the history of mysticism ; that history teems with examples of souls which, beginning well in some mystic state, have ended in delusion and ignominy. Their apologists do not usually blame them ; they are seldom shown to have been conscious hypocrites ; they have merely been deluded themselves and then have unconsciously deluded others. Clearly, then, it is for those who have begun to make headway in contemplation, and the contemplative life, that the Rule has been written. Having stated the fact of the danger, the author next describes how the delusion may come about. In the Fourth Rule he says :

> ' It is peculiar to the bad angel, who " transforms himself into an angel of light," to enter with the devout soul and take his own way out ; that is to say, to bring good and holy thoughts suitable to such a just soul, and afterwards, little by little, he tries to get his own way, bringing the soul into his hidden wiles and perverse intentions.'

The significance of this description is best understood when one has seen it in fact. May it not be said that the source of all heresy, and of all false mysticism, is due to a certain obstinacy, a holding to one's own opinion which one has convinced oneself is right, against the judgement of those who know better ? The soul has become acquainted with prayer ; it has leapt forward in its delights ; it has been shown a course, yet more full of these delights, which are most suited to its own nature. It has told itself that this indeed is the way of true contemplation, and nothing shall make it think otherwise ; when it has reached that stage then the ' transformed angel of light ' may hope to ' take his own way out.' And yet, the sincere and well-intentioned soul may protest, how is it to know the difference between true and false guidance ? How is it to distinguish between this transformed ' angel of light ' from the truly ' good angel ' ? St. Ignatius sets himself to answer these questions in the Rules that follow. And first, he would have the soul consider its own state, and the steps that have led up to this final subjective conviction. He writes :

> ' We ought to attend much to the course of the thoughts ; and if the beginning, middle, and end are all good, tending to all good, it is a sign of the good angel. But if the course of the thoughts which he brings ends in something wrong or distracting, or less good than that which the soul had before proposed to do, or which weakens or disquiets or disturbs the soul, depriving it of its peace, tranquillity, and quiet which it before possessed, it is a clear sign that it proceeds from the evil spirit, enemy of our profit and eternal salvation.'

Once more, the teaching of the saint is, at first sight, so platitudinous that one wonders what it contains. Obviously, if all in one's experience is good, its beginning and its end, if there has been no hesitation in the soul whatsoever, but all has led to a goal at which it has been wholly at peace with God, all is well and there is no more to say. But this is not always the experience. The most elementary form of prayer is full of what are called distractions ; sometimes these distractions lead, not only to wool gathering, but to conclusions that appal even the soul itself. Sometimes, again, a prayer that had begun in peace and hope ends in restlessness, in disgust, even in a kind of despair. The soul cannot at first account for it ; old temptations have come back, old doubts have reawakened, fresh reasons for being less spiritually ambitious have made it wonder and less happy in its new state. Can all be well ? Is it making a mistake ? And the soul, in the midst of the new confusion, begins to turn away from the light that leads it, to concentrate more upon itself, to ambition something ' less good than that which it had before proposed to do.'

Now in all these Rules it is important to notice how the saint dwells upon ' peace, tranquillity, and quiet of soul ' as the measure of all true progress, and to be preserved at all costs. So much does he wish the director to make of it that, in the Seventh Rule, he comes back to it, and describes it all again. In the first set of Rules he had said that those who go ' from mortal sin to mortal sin ' are soothed by the evil spirit and disturbed by the good one, while it is the contrary with those who are striving to be true. Here he renews the same Rule, but, as it were, the order is reversed, and the language is far more inspiring. The author is no longer speaking to those who are getting rid of their sins and beginning on the way of perfection ; he is addressing those who have already had experience of the light, who have delighted to run in the way of the commandments, who have determined to sorrow for their sins and to suffer in amendment ; and have found that their suffering has been turned into joy and gladness. They have asked themselves, Can all this be true ? Are they not being deceived ? Ought they not to be content with the ways of the penitent and not seek after the things that are more excellent but are not for them ? St. Ignatius knows what they fear. He has, therefore, pointed out what danger they might apprehend ; but never for a moment would he have them slacken in their effort after God, never would he have them lose any of that ' peace, tranquillity, and quiet ' which they have gained and which are the contemplative's characteristics. Whatever else they may fail to grasp in the Rules he has given they must not forget this. He seems almost to say : Keep joy in prayer and all will be well ; if you are spiritually unhappy then you may know that the enemy is near. One is struck by the repetition of this in various ways, not only in these Rules but in other parts of the Exercises. Thus, as if to put a last touch to this appeal, he writes in the Seventh Rule :

' In those who are advancing from well to better the good angel touches such a soul sweetly, lightly, and suavely, like a drop of water which enters a sponge ; and the bad angel touches him sharply, and with noise and disquiet, as when the drop of water falls on the stone. And those who are going on from bad to worse, the above mentioned spirits touch in a contrary manner, of which the cause is that the disposition of the soul is contrary to the said angels, or similar.

For when it is contrary they enter with noise and with commotion, perceptibly ;  and when it is similar they enter with silence, as into their own house by an open door.'

After all this, repeated and repeated, it would be impossible to say that St. Ignatius makes nothing, or even little, of spiritual consolations.  They are the gauge by which he judges progress, they are the chief thing to be watched that the soul may not be deceived.  All this second set of Rules are occupied with this one topic, and they are given to one who has begun the Illuminative Way, the Way of one who has begun to long to do something for God.  Having made these consolations so attractive and desirable he adds two characteristic hints for their better defence.  He has told us how the ' transformed angel ' will endeavour, ' little by little to get his own way ' ; he almost suggests that the soul at this stage will scarcely be tempted in any other way.  Sin, as such, will merely disgust him ; if he is to be led astray it must be under the appearance of good.  Hence it is not to be wondered at if, at times, the ' enemy ' partially succeeds.  The soul will answer to a light which will seem to it good.  There will come a time when it will doubt ; still there will seem no reason, or not sufficient reason, for changing, and it will go on.  The doubt increases ; the soul begins to be restless and unhappy ; it loses its ' sweetness and spiritual joy ' ; St. Ignatius says at once, without any reservation, that this alone is a sign that the light is untrue.  Let it go back ; let it, when the prayer is over, look and see where the deviation began, and what were the steps that led it astray. Let him make note of all this ; let him hence learn a little about himself and the weak places in his own defences—a loophole for vanity, it may be, or for self-indulgence, or for some other fault to enter in. Let him secure himself where he discovers the weaknesses ; above all, whatever happens, let him look to his union with and joy in the Lord. There is something almost naïve, a touch of humour, in the way he gives this warning :

'When the enemy of human nature shall have been felt and recognised by his serpent's tail and the evil end to which he leads on, it profits the person who was tempted by him to observe at once the course of the good thoughts which he brought to him, and the beginning of them, and how little by little he endeavoured to make him descend from the sweetness and spiritual joy in which he stood, until he brought him to his depraved intention, in order that with such experience understood and noted he may guard himself in future against his accustomed wiles.'

Still, for all its humour, it is precisely this Rule which reveals why elsewhere their author calls them all 'too subtle and too sublime for' the one less advanced 'to be able to understand.' The Rules against desolation, which are mainly those of the First Week, are easy enough, so he seems to say ; there the soul has only to stand firm and all will come right. But the Rules for consolation are more delicate ; there the soul is dealing with what is good, and it is not always easy to distinguish between the truly good, and that which is only apparent.

Even in that consolation which comes wholly from God, the 'infused' consolation of which he has already spoken, it is possible to be misled ; and this is the last warning which the saint suggests.  The realisation, consolation, contemplation, call it what we like, may come ' without cause,' from God only, and therefore it must be wholly good.  Still the sequel may err.  After the visitation is over the soul may add something of its own ;  it may seek to increase its fervour and devotion, in itself no mistake, and it may fail to recognise that the consolation is now on a lower plane.  It may form its own conclusions, thinking that these, too, are part of the revelation given to it by God.  Such conclusions may indeed be good ;  but also they may be false.  It may pass judgements on spiritual matters, it may make resolutions as to things to be done, which may be sound, but which may also be mistaken ;  there is scarcely a mystic, whether saint or not, but especially among the second class, from whose experiences this may not be illustrated.  This is the significance of the eighth and last Rule, the final warning, as it were, to any soul before he lets it go free along the highest path of contemplation.  Go by all means, he seems to say ;  it is precisely to this that the Exercises have led.  But when you go keep in mind this last word of guidance, given by one who has himself trodden the same path :

' When the consolation is without cause, although there be no deceit in it, as being solely from God Our Lord, as has been said ;  yet the spiritual person to whom God gives such consolation ought with much vigilance and attention to observe and to distinguish the very time of such actual consolation from the following time, in which the soul remains fervent and favoured with the favour and remnants of the consolation now past.   For oftentimes in this second time, by its own discourse in correlating concepts and judgements and drawing consequences from them, either by the action of the good spirit or of the bad, it forms various purposes and opinions which are not given directly by God Our Lord, and therefore have need to be examined very well before entire credit be given them or they be put into effect.'

There is one part of this last Rule for Discernment of Spirits which is usually overlooked, and yet which, if only because of its place at the end of all the Rules, would seem to be essential for the right understanding of the mind of St. Ignatius on prayer.   He is often spoken of as the saint of ' discursive meditation ' ; the ' method of St. Ignatius ' is said to be that of ' memory, understanding and will.'   Yet here, as the last thing for the man of prayer to bear in mind, it is explicitly said that such a method holds only at best a second place, and its conclusions are not to be wholly trusted.   The one true and infallible prayer is when God Himself speaks to the soul ; when He does not speak, when the soul must pray as best it is able, then ' oftentimes by its own discourse in correlating concepts and judgements and drawing consequences from them, it forms various purposes and opinions.'   Such conclusions may be good, but they are not the most sure.   They are inevitably mixed with something of our own, they are not

' given directly by God Our Lord.'  They must be
tested as such before they are accepted ;  they are
not to be confounded with the fruit of that higher
and better prayer to which he hopes every exercitant
who is faithful will attain.   To St. Ignatius at least,
' discursive prayer ' as it is called, if it is prayer at
all, is only prayer in default of something better.
If the soul receives no light, it must needs use its
own faculties, groping its way as well as it is able.
When the light goes out, it may again be reduced to
the same dependence upon itself.   But let it not be
mistaken ;  neither of these second states is to be
compared with the prayer, the light, which comes
from ' God Our Lord ' Himself.   That is ' the true
light which enlighteneth ' ;  the only one to be
wholly trusted ;  and though in the meditations and
contemplations that are to follow the author will
make much use of ' memory, understanding, and
will,' he tells us clearly beforehand how relative,
and only relative, is their importance in true prayer.

# V

## THE EXERCITANT

WE have thus seen that the Spiritual Exercises are, first and foremost in the mind of their author, exercises in prayer. We have seen that he looks for progress in prayer above all things else, and looks on this progress alone as the sure test of the soul's advance in the Exercises themselves. And thirdly, we have seen, that while the Exercises are intended to carry a soul along the way of prayer, showing it the steps and guarding it from pitfalls, still there comes a point where neither exercises nor the help of any man can be of any avail ; once the soul has come into union with God it must be left there for God Himself to teach it. Hence we have seen how the saint has turned from the subject of prayer to the director. In the advice given to him we notice chiefly words of warning. He must not be anxious to hear the exercitant's confession ; his chief business must be to watch the operations of his soul, the different spirits that affect him. He must not crowd the exercitant's mind with ' abundance of knowledge,' nor even with too many reasons, however good ; more important is it that the exercitant should ' see ' things for himself, should feel them, should have his whole being stirred by the discovery for himself of a new world. He must not try to influence the exercitant, one way or another ; indeed it would almost seem that his wisest course would be to leave the exercitant's resolutions alone altogether. All he has to do is to bring the soul, as soon as possible, and as close as possible, into direct union with God. When he has done that, when the soul and God are really brought together, then not only he should, but he must, step back ; his work is done, and God will do the rest. During all this time, work, the apostolate, or whatever else of the kind, have not been so much as mentioned ; never once have we been given any hint that St. Ignatius has in mind the making of anything more than a soul of the most intimate and the highest prayer ; and the only goal he has set before himself, the exercitant, and the director has been the attainment of the most intimate union with God. This brings joy and peace, and this alone ; a peace which the world cannot give, which no man can take away, which must be preserved at all costs, before man's place in the world is so much as considered.

This, then, is the primary purpose of the Exercises. It is to bring the Creator and His creature close together, so that they may speak the more familiarly and intimately with one another ; that the Creator may give Himself the more to His creature ; that He may fill it the more with an experienced knowledge of Himself ; that hence it may be drawn to love Him and praise Him the better; that it may spend the rest of its life in this love and praise, which is His service, that now and henceforth the Creator may deal directly with the creature, ' as friends are

wont to converse with each other ' ; that in the
same way, now and through all its life, the creature
should deal with its Creator and Lord as the one
Beloved whom at last it has found, and will never
again let go. So far as the Director of the Exercises
is concerned, this is the goal which ' it is more fitting
and far better ' that he should keep before himself,
leaving all the rest to God and the soul itself.
It is for him to make a soul of prayer, even a mystic
if the wherewithal is there, certainly a contemplative
so far as he is able. Should God wish that soul to do
otherwise, to ' dispose it ' in some other way ' to
serve Him in the future,' that is no business of the
director ; it is for God alone to ' choose whom He
will Himself,' and for the soul alone, under God's
guidance, to say its ' Ecce ancilla Domini.' It would
be difficult to find a more clear proof that the writer
of the Exercises was himself a contemplative of the
most intimate kind ; that, above all things else,
he would train a soul to the most intimate contemplation ; that, to him, all active work, no matter
how engrossing, was nothing more than the overflow of the fruit of contemplation on the rest of
mankind. His idea of life, contemplative or active,
is precisely the same as that of St. Teresa, who, as
a result of her contemplation, longed to ' go over
the whole world ' telling man of Jesus Christ. It is
the same as that of St. Thérèse of Lisieux, whose
zeal for souls has made her co-patron of the missions,
by the side of that son of St. Ignatius, Francis
Xavier. Thérèse was no less a missionary than
Xavier ; Xavier was no less a contemplative than
Thérèse ; had either been less the one, the one
would also have been less the other.

But the author of the Exercises is no theorist. He has built up his book of notes from experience, both of himself, and of others whom he has tried to train. He knows very well, first, that not everyone is capable of rising to the ideal he has drawn ; circumstances will interfere with some, ambitions with others, with some it will be sheer natural inability. Therefore before he concludes his preliminary remarks, his ' Annotations,' he must say something about those who may make the Exercises. His remarks are mainly of two kinds. First he speaks of certain hindrances which may belong to every soul, both the most and the least spiritually capable ; then he divides exercitants into classes or degrees, and sees what may be done for them. The hindrances are twofold ; difficulty in actual prayer, and attachment of some kind to one's own interests. Hence he gives two recommendations, the first of which is that the soul that would really learn to pray must train itself to spend in the ' exercise ' a whole hour, not less. It will be remembered that Louis of Granada and St. Peter of Alcantara, his contemporaries, put the limit at an hour and a half ; but both include in the time spiritual reading and preparation, which St. Ignatius does not. In pleading for the hour he says that

' the enemy '—how frequently already he has used this description !—' is wont to make no small effort to have the hour shortened.'

He does not tell us how, but experience tells us ; by distraction, the wandering of the mind, by the interference of outside affairs, by physical or mental weariness, sometimes by that utter blank which comes to those who are more advanced in prayer, as St. Teresa and St. John of the Cross teach. Against all these, St. Ignatius tells us, the mere holding on to the allotted time, lengthening it, if only for a minute, when the temptation comes to cut it short, is of great moment : this is confirmed by explanation.

' In time of consolation,' he tells us, ' it is easy and unburdensome to spend the whole hour in contemplation ' ;

and the whole context shows that what he means by ' contemplation ' in the sentence is precisely that which is meant by the mystics. When the soul is lost in that prayer which ' tastes and sees how sweet is the Lord,' it is easy to remain there : ' Lord it is good for us to be here.' But in what is it easy, and what is the soul doing all the time ?  Most certainly not reasoning, not ' discoursing ' ;  has there ever been a man who could find it ' easy and not burdensome to spend the whole hour ' in serious reasoning on any subject under the sun ?  Instead, at some moment of its prayer, perhaps at the very beginning, the mind has been raised up to God and it has seen. The heart has followed and it has loved. The two together have no longer needed to act, to ' make acts ' ;  they are wholly absorbed in the realisation of the truth of God and His Christ. Such prayer, once it has been stirred, is easy ;  and, as we may see, is encouraged by St. Ignatius beyond every other. Whenever the soul has arrived at that stage he will leave it there, bid it leave all else aside, and spend as much time in the ' relish ' of it as the good God will allow it. This is contemplation, the outgrowth, it may be, of reasoning but wholly transcending it ; the goal of every ' spiritual exercise ' and completing it ; to come to this prayer, to aim at it in every ' hour ' one devotes to prayer, is of the essence of the Exercises.

But the saint knows very well, first, that, apparently, not every soul can easily arrive at this permanent degree of prayer, but must usually plod along in faith, and hope, and effort ; second, that even those who rise to great heights of prayer have their violent reactions.  Sometimes, even for these, there will be long periods during which prayer becomes an utter blank ; sometimes, even in the midst of consolation, the whole of Thabor collapses beneath them, and they are left suspended in mid air, then prayer becomes doubly hard, and none is more tempted than the man of prayer to fear, to suspect, to doubt, and to set his prayer aside.  The ' enemy ' recommends him to leave it, at least for the time being, and produces many arguments to support him.

> ' In time of desolation it is difficult to complete the hour,'

says St. Ignatius with deep sympathy ;  and he gives advice which, in like circumstances, even St. Teresa, but not St. John of the Cross, seems to hesitate to give.  He writes :

> ' In order to struggle against the desolation, and to overcome the temptation, the exercitant ought always to remain at prayer rather more than the complete hour.'

And the purpose, the object to be gained, is :

' to accustom himself not only to resist the enemy, but even to overthrow him ' ;

the second giving the assurance that perseverance in such conquest will one day win its reward. Not only will the temptation to shorten prayer cease, but the soul, when it is free, will go to prayer by preference ; when it is not free, it will look forward to the hour of prayer as a haven of delight and rest.

Having thus secured prayer against its first danger, that of weariness and ennui, the saint next faces the second. The sixteenth of the Annotations is little less than a summary of the teaching developed later by St. John of the Cross in the *Ascent of Mount Carmel*. St. John in that book, which he considers to be an essential introduction to the others, teaches complete detachment, to an extent that alarms the reader, for the soul that would ascend high in the experience of God ; St. Ignatius likewise, less in detail, and perhaps for the present less severely, teaches the same.

' For this purpose,' he writes, ' that is to say, in order that the Creator and Lord may work more certainly in His creature, if perchance such a soul has an inordinate affection or inclination to anything, it is very expedient that it should exert itself with all its might to arrive at the contrary of that to which it is wrongly affected. For instance, if it has an inclination to seek or hold an office or benefice, not for the honour and glory of God Our Lord, or for the spiritual salvation of souls, but for its own private advantage

K

and temporal interests, it must incline itself to
the contrary, being instant in prayers and other
spiritual exercises, and begging God Our Lord
for the contrary, protesting, that is, that it does
not desire such an office or benefice or anything
else, unless His Divine Majesty, regulating its
desires, have changed its first affection ; so that
the cause of its wishing or holding one thing or
another may be solely the service, honour, and
glory of His Divine Majesty.'

Here again it is interesting to notice the means
by which the saint would bring about this detachment.  In some sense he asks for less than St. John ;
he is content to apply his doctrine to that which is
' inordinate.'  Nevertheless he knows human weakness ; hence he asks for no excessive will power, as
modern psychology would call it, but wholly for a
further use of prayer :  ' Being instant in prayers
and other spiritual exercises, and begging God Our
Lord for the contrary.'

We come, finally, to the consideration of those
for whom the saint supposes the Exercises to be
best suited.  No one can read the standard of prayer
which has already been described and believe that
St. Ignatius expected that anyone would attain it.
On the other hand he presumed that the Exercises
would be given only to one person at a time, in
which case perhaps anyone, if he would go through
them, would reach the goal he proposed ; in this
he would seem to agree entirely with the Dominican
teaching.  Moreover, in practice, great as were the
results of the Exercises on individuals like Peter
Faber, St. Francis Xavier, and others, yet even

these men were not specially selected by the saint.
They were the first that came his way, happening
to live with him in the same lodgings, and though,
no doubt, Providence had so arranged it for the
benefit of all, still St. Ignatius had taken just what
came first to his hand. Nevertheless not all had
been successes, and even among those whom he
had trained some had received the seed better
than others. He used to say later that none of his
disciples had understood the Exercises better, or
used them with better results, than his disciple
Peter Faber ; which alone would imply that he
had long discovered for himself different categories,
or degrees, of souls of prayer. Hence, before he
concludes his introductory notes, he has some
advice to give about those who make them.
Though in his book he has described an ideal, still

'the spiritual exercises should be adapted to
the dispositions of the persons who wish to
make them, that is to say, to their age, education, or intelligence, lest to one who is illiterate
or of weak constitution be given things which he
cannot easily bear or profit by. In the same
way, according as each desires to dispose himself,
that should be given whereby he will be the
better able to help himself and profit.'

Thus, in the first place there is a difference
caused by 'age, education, or intelligence'; by
'illiteracy,' or even 'weak constitution'; by the
purpose for which a man wishes to make a retreat,
'according as each desires to dispose himself.'
Secondly, the Exercises are to be given, not so
much to lighten the work of the exercitant, but

that he may ' help himself and profit,' and therefore
they must be such as he can ' easily bear and profit
by ' ; nothing beyond his reach, nothing that
merely leaves him passive. With these preliminary
warnings the saint divides those who make retreats
into different categories ; these categories are not
mutually exclusive, but they are meant to serve as
a guide. Moreover, they throw much light on the
use St. Ignatius intended for his book ; and that
less from what he says than from what he does not
say. However high the ideal he has set before us,
he hopes that there is no type of sincere servant of
' God Our Lord ' whom they may not be made to
help. These categories, then, are :

(1) ' He who wishes to help himself in order to
be instructed and to arrive at a certain degree of
contentment of soul ' ; in other words, that excellent type of exercitant met usually in ordinary lay
retreats ;

(2) ' He who is a poor subject or of little natural
capacity, so that not much fruit can be hoped for
from him ' ; yet even such a soul must not be
despised ;

(3) He who ' is involved in public affairs or
suitable business, whether he be a man of letters
or of talent ' ; one, in other words, who is the opposite to the last, but whose life in the world has
fixed for him his vocation and must be his chief
preoccupation ;

(4) He who ' is more free and wishes to profit to
the utmost.'

For each of these St. Ignatius has a definite
course to suggest ; a study of his plans will show
both how well he adapts the spiritual life to different

needs and yet has always in mind the very highest ambitions of all. Taking the second of these categories first :

(1) For ' poor subjects and those of little capacity ' he recommends :

(i) ' easy exercises until they have confessed their sins ' ;

(ii) ' some examinations of conscience and a plan for confessing more often than was their custom ' ;

(iii) ' so as to preserve themselves in what they have gained.'

This, perhaps, is the ideal aimed at in general parochial missions.

(2) For ' those who wish to help themselves in order to be instructed and to arrive at a certain degree of contentment of soul ' :

(i) ' the particular examination,'

(ii) ' the general examination,'

(iii) ' for half an hour in the morning the method of prayer on the commandments, mortal sins,' etc.

(iv) ' confession of sins once a week,'

(v) ' the Sacrament (Holy Communion) once a fortnight, or better, if he be moved thereto, every week.'

Perhaps none of the four categories is more confirmed by practical experience than this. In ordinary retreats to laymen, for instance, to our working men, nothing goes more home than sinlessness of life on the one hand and frequentation of the sacraments on the other. Other things may be added, but almost instinctively the giver of the retreat will direct them to one or other of these.

(3) For ' those involved in affairs or business,' assuming that such men can give, perhaps, two hours a day to the Exercises and no more, but that spread over a considerable time, he makes three divisions :

   (i) Consideration of the End of Man, with the Examinations of Conscience, Confession, and Communion.

   (ii) Considerations of Sin and its Consequences.

   (iii) The Mysteries of Christ.

This third class is one that has become more or less obsolete, though why it should have done so is not clear. Its nearest representative is, perhaps, in the retreats given to sodalities of men in active life, Children of Mary, etc., when a meditation may be given in the morning before they go to work, and again in the evening, after the day's work is done. For these, as with the others, the suggestions can only be directive, not prescriptive ; above all since among such exercitants there are many, perhaps most, who, though not free, yet truly ' wish to profit to the utmost,' that is, in spirit at least, belong to the fourth class.

(4) But it is upon this fourth class upon which the saint concentrates. It need not consist of priests or religious ; he asks for only two conditions when he says :

   ' When a man is more free and wishes to profit to the utmost all the spiritual exercises in their proper order are to be given, in the same order in which they proceed.'

This he asks for from the beginning ; a sincere desire to do one's best, ' with great courage and generosity towards his Creator and Lord,' as he has said elsewhere already, and ' offering to Him all his will and freedom.' He does not wish to spend the time of the retreat in merely stirring up the desire to be brave and generous ; he assumes at least the desire to be true and sincere. Such a man he recommends to withdraw into solitude, separating himself from friends and acquaintances, from all worldly care and attraction, even from the house or room in which he usually lives ; and this, primarily, for a purpose which takes us by surprise, that he may the more easily go to Mass and Vespers. He directs :

' Wherein, as a rule, he will benefit in proportion as he withdraws himself from all his friends and acquaintances, and from all worldly care ; as for example if he leaves the house in which he was staying and takes another house or room in order to dwell therein in all possible secrecy, so that it may be in his power to attend Mass and Vespers daily without fear of being hindered by his acquaintances.'

So that ' Mass and Vespers daily,' in other words the daily liturgical services, are part of the Exercises of St. Ignatius ! How much he made of these is shown sufficiently in his own early life at Manresa. Yet for what purpose, seeing that the liturgy is in no way connected with the Exercises' supposed specific purpose ? Surely the answer is contained in the first definition, given long ago on the first page of his book : ' every method of vocal and mental prayer.' No kind of 'vocal' prayer can compare with the liturgy ; none more 'raises the mind and heart to God ' ; to live by the liturgy is to live in the atmosphere of the angels, who sing 'Sanctus, sanctus, sanctus,' for all eternity. To live in such an atmosphere cannot but have its effect upon all other prayer ; so that when the soul returns to that perhaps inferior kind of prayer, the study of itself, it does so all the more in the sight and the hearing of the messengers of God. It is remarkable that Peter Faber, from the time that he made the Exercises, cultivated this devotion to the angels, seeing them about him wherever he went.

Still, when St. Ignatius speaks of 'Mass and Vespers ' it seems evident that he uses these merely as an illustration ; we are accustomed to his substituting a particular example for a general principle. He is chiefly concerned with the ' withdrawal ' of the exercitant from his ' friends and acquaintances, and from all worldly care.' It is his aim, so far as it is possible, to lift the soul, for the time being, out of this life altogether, so that nothing at all, not the smallest trifle, should tie him to it. For once, he seems to say, even if nothing else comes of the retreat, let us give ' God Our Lord ' these few days of absolute and entire love and service. Let us see how far, by shutting ourselves off from everyone and everything else, we can praise and serve ' God Our Lord ' with our whole heart and our whole soul if only for a day. Such an act of genuine generosity, short as it is, ' merits not a little in the sight of His Divine Majesty ' ; such whole-hearted devotion, whatever may come of it, cannot but be pleasing to God. But that will not be all; let it but be whole-hearted and it will inevitably lead to something else. Even in the natural order concentration on one subject, with all distractions removed, gives the mind more freedom; much more in the supernatural order, to use the saint's own words, one who

> ' places his care on one thing alone, that is to say, on the serving of his Creator, and the profit of his own soul, uses his natural powers more freely in seeking with diligence what he so much desires.'

Solitude, we hear him say, with no material trammel intervening, gives vision of the super-natural. Solitude quickens the spiritual hearing, so that one catches far more readily the lessons of spiritual understanding. Solitude enables the soul to ' taste and see how sweet is the Lord.' But most of all, and this the saint puts down as its third and chief ' advantage,'

> ' the more our soul finds itself alone and secluded, the more it renders itself fit to approach and draw near to its Creator and Lord; and the more it thus draws near, the more it prepares itself to receive graces and gifts from His divine and supreme bounty.'

It will be noticed that this sentence, the closing sentence of the Annotations, like so many sentences with which St. Ignatius concludes certain sections, is a general statement. It refers, not only to the Exercises, or only to the time of retreat, but to the whole of life. It is not a special conclusion, it is an axiom ; he who hopes for greater union and conversation with his ' Creator and Lord ' will cultivate solitude. It is the last encouragement of the saint to the soul that would go far ; and yet, as it stands, it is no more than a summary of the Carthusian ideal. It is, wholly and without equivocation, a defence of, and an inducement to, the contemplative life ; ' the more our soul finds itself alone and secluded ' the more perfect in itself it becomes before God, ' the more it renders itself fit to approach and draw near to its Creator and Lord.' Still further, the more completely the soul aims at the life of contemplation, the more does it prepare itself for the highest and most intimate graces of ' His divine and supreme bounty,' especially for that greatest of all, the knowledge and experience of union with Him. This is the climax as St. Ignatius sees it, and as he puts it before both director and exercitant, when as yet he has given not a single meditation, or contemplation, or other spiritual exercise. It is, as usual, a great advance on what he said at the beginning. Then he told us that the Exercises were to be made ' to dispose the soul to rid itself of all disordered affections, and after having got rid of them, to seek and find the divine will in the disposition of one's life.' Now he points indefinitely higher. Make the Exercises, he says, and you will gain all this and much more. You will see, you will taste, you will approach consciously near to your Creator and Lord. You will make yourself ready for the most signal graces He may be pleased to grant you ; and what those graces are ' eye hath not seen, nor ear heard, neither hath it entered into the heart of man to conceive.' St. Ignatius may have wished to make apostles ; but he would make them, first of all, by training them to be contemplatives.

Looking back on the Annotations, and taking with them the two sets of Rules for the Discernment of Spirits, one cannot fail to notice several things. First, the author assumes that prayer, and prayer alone, shall be the basis of all the Spiritual Exercises ; second, that his readers know what is meant by prayer, so much so that there is no need to discuss it in itself ; third, that in proportion as prayer progresses so far do the Exercises themselves progress. Finally, when the soul is perfect, that is, entirely self-surrendered out of love, then will its prayer also be perfect ; when it has given to its Creator all that it has and all it is then it may be humbly confident that its Creator and Lord will give to it in return His own self in perfect union. The author of the Exercises makes no exceptions ; he assumes from the beginning that so it will be ; the highest forms of prayer belong to no chosen few.

Hence the introductory Annotations, wholly and entirely, with scarcely a thought of anything else, concentrate on making the exercitant's prayer as perfect a thing as possible. First, he himself is warned not to allow the intellect to interfere too much with the action of the will ; to keep himself vividly in the presence of ' God Our Lord,' and to behave himself accordingly, that is, with becoming reverence ; to be brave and generous, to be firm in resisting temptations against prayer, to shut himself off that his Creator and Lord may possess him

entirely. Second, the director is also warned that
the giving of points is not the same thing as the
giving of a lecture ; that it is his chief business,
not to interfere, but to bring the soul and its Creator
more and more intimately in touch with one
another ; that he should study his exercitant, not to
know his sins as a confessor, but to be able to guide
him wholly and entirely in the way of prayer.
Third, with regard to the prayer itself ; in the
first place, because it is what it is, a whole-hearted
effort of the creature to reach its Creator, it will
inevitably incur opposition on the part of ' the
enemy of our human nature.' Second, that the
way to overcome that enemy will be by more rather
than less : more time given to prayer rather than
less, more self-oblation, more intimacy with Him
who makes all things co-operate to good, by withdrawal from everything else. Third, he reminds
the soul that there are the three degrees, phases,
or whatever one likes to call them, of prayer and
the spiritual life. There is prayer of purification,
making the soul clean of heart that it may see God.
There is prayer of illumination, that seeing it may
come to know, love, and, as he puts it, ' approach
and draw near.' There is, lastly, prayer of union,
which neither the soul nor its director can procure,
but which, for him who does what he is able, may
be confidently hoped for ' from His divine and
supreme bounty.'

In addition to all this, perhaps more important
than all else, besides his assumption about prayer,
besides his care that prayer shall be made as
perfectly and fruitfully as possible, the saint quite
simply reveals his own attitude towards it. Prayer,

to him, is not merely one of the things, not even the most important of the things, one looks to every day of one's life ; it is life itself, it lies beneath everything else, so that everything else, springing from it, becomes one continuous prayer. Thus the contemplative and the man of action are to him one and the same ; as the contemplative, being only human, cannot always actually pray, but as a break must plough his field or cut his harvest, so neither can the man of action always act, but must pray and fill his soul with prayer. It is no question of difference, it is a question only of more or less ; both alike seek first the kingdom of God and His justice, and then let Him dispose of them as He will.

Secondly, and in the same spirit of simplification, though he accepts and makes use of the three ' ways ' in the ascetical life, still he makes little or no difference in the ways of prayer ; though later he may offer different methods of awakening the soul, still prayer, as prayer, is the same. He would, perhaps, for the sake of scientific discussion, or of instruction, allow such distinctions as are made between the ' kinds ' of prayer, but there is no sign anywhere that he allows them in practice. In what is called the Prayer of Union he does not wait till a soul has reached what is called the Unitive Way ; he is prepared for his Creator and Lord to give it to a soul at any time, even at the beginning of its course, when it is still overwhelmed with the sense of its own wretchedness. Though he will present his material for ' meditation or contemplation ' after the manner of what is called ' discursive prayer,'—for how can he do otherwise?—yet always, at any point, not only does he bid the soul set all reasoning aside the moment it hears the voice of God, but he bids it listen for that voice, follow its call in preference to every other, be led to the bleeding feet of Christ and lose itself there, even while it is astonished that the world in indignation does not swallow it up. Two things only he insists upon : first, that the soul that would pray should use every means in its power to pray well, for he has no use for dilettante prayer ; and second, that, even so, growth in prayer, what some call degree in prayer, depends entirely on the great generosity of God. But this makes no real distinction, so far at least as the soul itself is concerned. Should it please God to lift up the soul, meditation may at any moment become the most sublime contemplation ; conversely, should He choose to leave it to itself, to the use of its own understanding, the most intense contemplation may become the feeble prayer which is all that man of himself can make. In all this he differs in nothing at all from the great contemplatives—a better and a safer word than mystics—both before his time and after him ; he has absorbed, from books and spiritual guides, what has gone before, and has passed it on to those who have come after, as is plain to see. If there is a difference it is only this : that whereas some of the great contemplatives, acting usually under obedience, have endeavoured to describe their experiences in the state of contemplation, Ignatius has been content to point the way to that state, to train the soul that it may reach it, leaving the results in the hands of the loving and generous Creator and Lord. He has, perhaps, feared to dazzle the soul's eyes with the glitter of graces not yet received ; he has preferred to hide the secret of the King. Instead he has spoken to the sinner of his sins, to the man of action of his duty ; yet all the time he has shown himself prepared to find at any moment the soul of ' large heart and generosity,' whether of sinner or of labourer, lifted into the heavens and conversing with its ' Creator and Lord,' even as was that of the sinner Saul, or of the fisherman Peter, or of James and John the sons of thunder.

# VI

# THE FIRST STAGE OF PRAYER

IN four places in the Annotations the author
has spoken of the divisions he proposes to make
in the Exercises. In the fourth he has said that
' the first is the consideration and contemplation
of sins ' ;

and has described its end in the words,

'Some are slower in attaining what they seek, that
is to say, contrition, sorrow, and tears for their sins.'

In the Ninth Annotation he has spoken of the
temptations most likely to beset a soul in this first
stage, and the way it should be treated :

' When the exercitant is engaged in the exercises
of the first week, if he be a person inexperienced
in spiritual matters, and if he be grossly and
openly tempted, as by alleging difficulties to his
advance in the service of God Our Lord, such as
labours, shame, and fear of losing worldly
honours, etc. ; let not him who gives the exercises
speak to him of the rules about the different
spirits belonging to the second week, for they
will injure him as much as the rules of spirits of
the first week will benefit him, the matter contained being too subtle and too sublime for him
to be able to understand.'

Thirdly, in the Tenth Annotation, he uses the technical terms of the ascetical theologians, the only place in the book, when he speaks of

'the illuminative life, which corresponds to the exercises of the second week,' and 'the purgative life, which corresponds to the exercises of the first week.'

Lastly, in the Eleventh Annotation, he confines, as it were, the scope of the exercitant in the first stage, to secure his greater success :

'It will be an advantage to one who is making the exercises of the first week, that he should know nothing whatever of what he is to do in the second week, but that he should work during the first week to attain what he seeks, as though he had no hope of finding anything good in the second.'

From these four remarks it is fairly clear what the saint has in mind when he sets out on his first stage. He is dealing with one who is not too experienced in prayer, but who, nevertheless, is in real earnest to be what God wants him to be and to do what God wants him to do.  He means to stir that soul, first to a keen desire for, and then to an attainment of, 'contrition, sorrow, and tears for its sins.'  There is nothing here said about confession, nothing about purpose of amendment in resolutions ;  the author concentrates on the soul itself, and the affections it will evoke, leaving the consequences to follow.  He therefore arranges his first Exercises with this end in view, and for such a soul ;  he adapts for it the prayer he means to give it.  It shall not be mere self-examination with a view to confession ;  this

L

he places entirely outside the series of the Exercises, assuming that the soul will attend to this, naturally and of its own accord. Though even here he gives it principles, and rules according to which it can work, drawn from his own experience, still he does not introduce the subject in his series ; he only adds in one place that

> ' the general confession will be better made immediately after the exercises of the first week,'

though this is only said after the warning,

> ' the general confession, for one who voluntarily wishes to make it,

as if, however ' advantageous ' such a confession may be—and he enumerates these ' advantages '—still even that is not an integral part of the Exercises. It is a corollary, an almost natural sequel to what he will have to say ; he puts it, therefore, not in the series, but as a preliminary note before he begins.

Moreover, there is nothing peculiarly ' Ignatian ' in Confession or Examination of Conscience ; when he turns the latter into a form of prayer, he does but set in order what is done by everyone for himself. More peculiar to him are what are styled the ' preludes ' to meditation. Without considering that precisely the same are to be found approved by other masters of the spiritual life, Louis of Granada, Peter of Alcantara, John of the Cross, it is more profitable to be sure that we know what they mean. Read them coldly as they stand, as a student may read a scientific treatise, and one will find little in them to induce to prayer, any more than one will find prayer in a proposition of Euclid. But read the words with the mind of him who wrote them, as has been described in the foregoing pages, and at once their meaning is clear. The First Exercise begins with a preparatory prayer.

' The preparatory prayer is to ask grace of God Our Lord that all my intentions, actions, and operations may be ordered purely to the service and praise of His Divine Majesty.'

Already in the Annotations the saint has stressed the importance of 'reverence' when we actually pray.

' In the acts of the will,' he has said, ' when we speak vocally or mentally with God Our Lord or with His saints, greater reverence is required on our part than when we are using the reason for understanding.'

But now he at once goes further ; he makes this ' reverence ' an integral part of every meditation, and that from the first moment. Who does not know the importance of recollection, of steadying the mind beforehand, for any sustained or prolonged prayer, such as, from the very first Exercise, St. Ignatius puts before the exercitant ? Some would say that they prefer to begin without any such preliminary ; we would suggest that for shorter prayer this may be very well, but few souls can plunge headlong into prayer that is to occupy an hour, and find that much of the time has not been wasted. Many, on the other hand, say they cannot meditate ; perhaps they only mean, if they knew it, that they have not taken the first step towards it. They have plunged into it, they have not steadied the mind in the actual presence of the living and

loving God. We are studying St. Ignatius as a
teacher of prayer, and this is his first lesson. Let a
soul only practise this every time it stands or kneels
to pray, let it make this a habit of prayer, and it
will not be long before it discovers from its own
experience the meaning of meditation and contemplation, far better than any book on the theory of
prayer can teach it. Such is the value of the preparatory prayer which, as the saint says, must never
be omitted in the Exercises ; in other words during
the whole period of training. So insistent is he upon
it that he will not be content with giving the direction once for all ; he repeats it with every meditation. And the reason is clear ; its purpose reaches
much further than the meditation it introduces.
This initial concentration on the actual presence of
' God Our Lord ' is itself a kind of contemplation
in brief, whatever else may follow. It is a lesson in,
and a step towards, even sublime prayer, which will
adapt itself to the soul that says it with attention ;
the time may come when, occasionally at least, it
will suffice for the whole hour of prayer, lifting the
soul up to the arms of the Father, from whom all
good things come, to whom all service flows, for
whom alone it is worth while to live.

But it is in what is called the First Prelude that
many see, and tend to complain of, what is known
as the Ignatian method.

' The first prelude is a composition, seeing the
place. Here it is to be noticed that in a contemplation, or visible meditation, such as contemplating Christ Our Lord, who is visible, the
composition will be to see with the sight of the

imagination the corporeal place where is found the object that I wish to contemplate. I say the corporeal place, such as a temple or a mountain where is found Jesus Christ or Our Lady, according to what I wish to contemplate.'

In this short passage, which has been the subject of much controversy if not of repudiation, we have more than one key to the mind of St. Ignatius. In the first place, here more than anywhere else in his book, we find his definition of 'contemplation.' 'Contemplation' to him is 'visible meditation'; and he gives as an example, 'contemplating Christ Our Lord, who is visible.' Now in all the writings of St. Teresa nowhere is she more bold than when she defends the 'visible' Christ, the Christ of the Gospel record, as the centre of all true contemplation, in opposition to those who would eliminate the Sacred Humanity that they may address their prayer to God alone. So bold is she that she seems almost to fear that she has gone too far ; she has contradicted theologians greater than herself, and apologises to them, but none the less she ends where she began. The Sacred Humanity, she maintains—and what canonised mystic does not?—is the object, or the channel, of the Christian's sublimest contemplation ; through Him, and with Him, and in Him we rise to that beyond which human reason, and prayer founded on human effort only, can never hope to reach.—'No man cometh to the Father but by me.'—'He that seeth me, seeth the Father also.' —There is a knowledge of God, sublime of its kind, which even the pagan unbeliever may reach ; such knowledge has often found beautiful expression

in the poetry of the East.   But, sublime as it is, it is
limited in its scope ;  it is the fruit of philosophy and
no more ;  its very fascination lies in the fact that it
is an expression of sublime ideas ;  only dimly, and
as it were on another plane from ours, does it
come in actual contact with human life.   It is
beautiful, it may be noble, but beyond cultivating
the philosophic outlook it has little influence on the
human soul.   Not so the knowledge of God that has
come to us through Christ.   We have learnt through
Him a new concept, a new vision, of the Father ;
for to see Christ is to see the Father also.   We see,
we hear, we feel, as St. John so emphatically repeats ;
and such knowledge of Him, real, personal, visible
with the eyes of the mind, is the key to a yet fuller
knowledge of God than any philosophy can give us,
is the key to the highest contemplation.   Leave
Christ Our Lord out of prayer and at first it may
seem that the soul rises free into the empyrean ;
but there comes a point where it can go no further,
it turns round and round in its own circle, and it
will be well if it does not fall back to earth.   Bring
in Christ and it is very different.   The progress may
at first seem to be slower ;  it took the apostles some
time to discover ' Christ the Son of the living God '
in the Man with whom they ate, and walked, and
slept ;  but the vision is the deeper, the knowledge is
at once more human and divine, in the end it leads
to infinity, not merely to the end of the earth.   It is
the contemplation that alone is found in the Gospels,
St. Peter, St. Paul, and St. John.

This was the kind of contemplation which first
captured Inigo Loyola when he lay on his bed of
sickness and read the Dominican-turned-Carthusian,

Ludolph of Saxony. He read for his amusement ;
the vision grew to a reality ; he saw Christ walking
the lanes and preaching in the synagogues ; later
he walked down those same lanes and entered those
synagogues, in search of Him whom he had learnt
to know and love. He discovered that, for us
human beings with our human limitations, a man
is best understood when seen in his surroundings ;
this is the meaning of biography, of the insertion
of some tiny detail which will reveal the whole man,
perhaps even more it is the genius of the portrait
painter, who by some trifling addition will tell us a
whole character at a glance. Hence, as a preliminary to prayer, as a ' prelude ' to the contemplation of Him who was the centre of all prayer, the
place, the circumstances, the conditions in which
that Humanity revealed itself, are, if not absolutely
essential, at least most valuable for the understanding of Jesus Himself. For no other reason do
scholars spend their years in studying the surroundings of the Gospel ; to know more of Bethlehem
and Nazareth, of Capharnaum and Jerusalem, of
Thabor and Calvary and the Mount of Olives, of
the synagogues in Galilee and the Temple in
Jerusalem, of the pastures on the hill-sides and the
shops in the streets, all this helps us the more to
know Him who grew up among them, who set us
an example in just such surroundings, whose words
and actions, and therefore Himself, are often to be
understood only by their means. One has seen it
written that the ' method ' of St. Ignatius gives us
a deeper insight into the Gospels but no more. It is
exactly the opposite ; it is preliminary insight into
the Gospels which sets his ' method ' into motion ;

when it has done that, then the living contemplation
begins, then Jesus comes to life before me, walks
out of the picture to me, and takes up His abode
in the place where I live.  To know Jesus Christ, my
companion with me while I pray, is much indeed ;
but I shall know Him as He was and is far better,
and love Him for it far more, when I have seen Him
with my own eyes, walking the streets He walked,
praying on the mountain-side, touching the sick
as He blessed them along the lane that led across
Genesareth.    This is the significance, not of a
' composition of place,' which suggests merely
inventive imagination, but of a ' composition, seeing
the place,' which are the saint's own words, and
express reality.    For those whose contemplation
is a life, and not merely spiritual speculation, it
brings Jesus Christ Our Lord before us, as He
stood before Simon Peter, teaching us, as He taught
him, to say : ' Lord, to whom shall we go ?  Thou
hast the words of eternal life. . . . Thou art the
Christ, the Son of the living God.'   And when we
have said that with our whole hearts, to One who
stands before us, absorbing us so that we forget our
own petty surroundings, then we have opened the
door to divine contemplation.  We have arrived at
a knowledge which flesh and blood have not
revealed to us, but our Father who is in heaven.
Jesus then Himself takes us out of the place in which
we found Him, up the mountain, and there is
transfigured before us.    Then we shall hear the
more clearly the voice of the Father Himself, even
though it come from the impenetrable cloud :
' This is my beloved Son, in whom I am well
pleased.  Hear ye him.'

Such is the purpose of a ' composition, seeing the place ' in what St. Ignatius calls ' visible meditation,' which is the beginning of ' contemplation.' But if it is effective for ' visible meditation,' no less may it be for the ' invisible.' For instance, he would have us take sin. The mere thought of sin, its definition, its abstract analysis, the decisions of moral theology concerning it, will usually have little effect upon the soul ; even reasoning about it, or threatening of punishment because of it, will often stir only anger and defiance. But let the sin-stained soul see itself in some way, not exaggeratedly but as it is actually, even in its own esteem, and the effect will be different. When it realises its actual foulness, its degradation, the loathsome condition of the soul stained by sin, there may be hope of some disgust and abhorrence. Sin has its grip upon mankind precisely because this truth is hidden from the eyes of men ; it is pictured to man as pleasant, as desirable, as in some way good ; the reality, with its consequences, is ignored. If then the soul can by some ' composition seeing the place ' be made to see the facts as they are, it is not unreasonable that one who would help it to set itself free from the deception and tyranny should use it. Sin declares that it makes man free ; every man knows in his heart that it enslaves. Sin says it is progress ; every man knows it is rottenness and corruption. Sin says it is a mark of manliness, and tells a man ' to be a man ' and not fear ; every man knows quite well that it is precisely sin that destroys the manhood in him, and makes him a brute beast. Sin, when convicted, would confine itself to the thing done, and would pass on to something else ; every man knows that evil done cannot be ignored so easily, it has affected his ' whole substance, soul and body.'

Hence, when St. Ignatius would give the sinner, —and who is not ?—a ' composition, seeing the place ' for this abstract thing, sin, he does no more than put before him the guilty sinner as he is. Let a man look at the fact, shorn of the bragging nonsense it affects, and with which it struts about : ' fair without, but within rottenness and dead men's bones.' It can, possibly, deceive men ; it cannot deceive the eye of Truth. Let a sinner see himself, not a free man, but imprisoned within himself ; not a better man for his sin, but in his corrupted body ; not manly because of it, but exiled among and reduced to the level of the beasts ; not just committing sin and moving on, but injured by it in his whole self, in body and in soul. To one who will make such a ' composition,' such a picturing of the fact, it may almost seem that there is no more to be done. ' Look on this picture and on that ' ; on the actual thing to which sin has reduced him, as compared with that which he might have been had he never sinned. If that is enough, if the soul can stay there in ' contemplation,' be it so ; but the ' meditation ' that follows may help to drive the revelation further home.

' The composition will be to see with the imaginative sight, and to consider my soul to be imprisoned in this corruptible body, and the whole substance to be in this valley, as though exiled among brute animals. I say the whole substance, soul and body.'

This, for the first Exercise and those that follow

in the considerations on sin, is the ' composition,
seeing the place ' and its significance.   There is no
further change ;   all that will be done will be to
look at the fact, and let the soul ' feel and relish
interiorly ' its truth.   It is not unnatural, it is not
exaggerated ;   so far at least there has been little
use of the reasoning faculty ;   the soul has been
asked to ' contemplate ' facts as they are, in themselves and in the sight of God.   There follows the
' second prelude,' which, for one who will be in
no hurry with his prayer,—and hurried or con-
tracted prayer never leads to anything,—is no less
natural than the first.   Every soul comes to prayer
wanting something ;   it may not know what that
' something ' is, it may ' know not what it asks for
when it prays,' but it longs and desires nevertheless ;
and often, for very many indeed, the whole of
prayer consists in the expression of that desire and
longing.—' My   God,   I   want.'—' What   do   you
want ? '—' I know not what I want, but I want.'—
In how many is this the prayer of their whole lives !
Beautiful and powerful prayer, truly contemplative
prayer, though such souls, because they seem to get
no farther, think they do not pray at all.   It is this
natural and primary longing of the soul that St.
Ignatius seizes on in his Second Prelude.   In the
first he has captured the first movements of the
mind, in the second he captures the first movements
of the heart :

> ' The second prelude is to ask of God Our Lord
> that which I want and desire.'

Naturally ' what I want and desire ' will not
always be the same.   It will grow with the soul's

growth ; it will be affected by the subject-matter
of the meditation ; or rather the other way about,
the matter of the meditation will be chosen according to ' what I want and desire.' Joyful subjects will
tend to make me rejoice ; sorrowful subjects will
lead me to sorrow ; and conversely when ' I want
and desire ' to rejoice I will choose some joyful
subject, when ' I want and desire ' to increase my
sorrow I will choose accordingly. Here the meditation is of sin, the very mention of which rouses a
sense of shame in any honest man, of confusion
and concealment if he knows himself to be guilty.
Or rather, not only ' if ' ; such is human nature that
there is little question of an ' if ' ; ' in multis
peccavimus omnes,' and the lives of most of us are
spent in hiding the shame and confusion, not only
from other eyes, for that is usually easy, but also
from our own. We do not like to know we are
as guilty as we are ; we do not want to be so shamed,
even to ourselves. Therefore, if I wish to be
genuine, if I would be a true man, inside and out,
independently of what I may appear, which is just
what the worldling, with all his boasting, does not
wish to be, is too great a coward to be, then I will
' want and desire ' to act accordingly. I will not
merely talk glibly about sin, I will not merely
contemplate the picture of its crawling slime, I
will not argue with myself about it and call that
' meditation.' I will do much more ; I will see
its truth in myself and take the consequences. I
will ask God, without whom I can do nothing, to
give me this realisation of the truth of myself ; to
fill me with true shame and confusion because of
the true fact, and not to play the hypocrite, at

least with myself; to realise how much disgrace
I have justly deserved, how others have been justly
made to pay the penalty of their misdeeds and I
have not.

' Here it will be to ask for shame and confusion
at myself, seeing how many have been marred
through a single mortal sin, and how often I
have deserved to be condemned for ever for my
so many sins.'

When the two preludes are so interpreted one
might at first say that they are a ' meditation or
contemplation ' in themselves ; that their realisation is all that is needed to elicit a perfect act of
contrition. There is much in this ; one may add,
as has already been hinted, that the rest of the
Exercise will not carry us much further. It will
help to know ' interiorly ' the opening truth ; it
will not teach us much more. In matter of fact,
when we listen to the most impressive mission sermons, or when we read such convincing preachers
as Segneri, St. John Vianney, perhaps, too, such
as St. Bernardine of Siena, one may ask whether
they attempt to go any further. This at least is
certain, that few if any great mission preachers
omit them, or can afford to do so. They must
make sin real, they must picture the fact, and the
fact must appeal to the sense of justice in their
hearers. But in prolonged private prayer, where
the words and descriptions of another do not give
the hearer occupation, unless these two preludes
are otherwise developed they will lose their hold.
It is true they contain in germ the whole of the
' meditation or contemplation,' but they must be

suffered to grow; above all for a soul that is only
just beginning to think and pray for itself; something must be done for it that it may see and feel
more. This is what is meant by 'points' for
meditation.

This leads us at once to the vexed question of
what is called 'discursive' meditation, that new
word, recently invented, of which in times past I
think there is no trace. It is a word almost invariably used with a certain condescending approval,
but also with more than a hint that those who
practise it do not really know what prayer is at
all. Their prayer is 'discursive,' that is it partakes
of the nature, not of prayer, but of a discourse.
Such men of prayer turn prayer into 'discoursing,'
and they teach, not how to pray, but how to think
out a sermon. This, at least, is more than hinted
at by some who emphasise the phrase 'discursive
meditation'; and the Exercises of St. Ignatius,
useful as no doubt they are for 'preaching' a
retreat, are altogether useless as a guide to prayer.
Such is the assumption, and its foundation is the
so-called 'Ignatian method' of 'memory, understanding, and will,' of 'persons, words, and
actions.' Evidently, it is said, by these two methods
St. Ignatius made 'reasoning' more important than
'prayer'; indeed he uses the very word, bidding
us to 'discourse more in detail with the understanding' in the first Exercise, and that three times
over, once in each of the points. His 'method' is
admirable for the making of strong-minded men
and men of action; but it does not conduce to
making men of prayer.

Enough will have been said already to show that if this is true then St. Ignatius has either frustrated his own object, or has been mistaken in the use of his machinery ; he meant to make a man of prayer and he has only turned out a ' soldier.' Before analysing the meaning of his ' method ' we would suggest that St. Ignatius was not the man to have made such a mistake ; that he was himself a contemplative and mystic of the truest type ; and that the results of his training were men of prayer, far above anything else. But what is prayer ? It is the ' raising of the mind and heart to God ' ; in other words, the raising of the whole soul to God, with all its faculties. If I recall God to my mind, if I ' remember ' God, I pray ; if I dwell upon Him, realising, knowing Him, I pray ; if my heart goes out to Him and I want Him, I pray ; and the most contemplative saint will acknowledge that any one of these, not only is a true method of prayer, but is a method which, if blessed by God, may lead and has led to the sublimest prayer. The ecstasies of St. Teresa seem to have come, not so much from any act of the will, for often, as she tells us, she used her will to try to prevent them, and almost always encouraged her daughters to do the same. Ecstasies were not to be sought, on the contrary they were to be suspected ; such was the attitude towards them she regularly taught, however much she experienced them in herself. In her case almost always, they came to her in spite of herself ; for instance, from a mere act of memory and recollection when, as she came into choir, she recalled the presence of God (the preliminary prayer of St. Ignatius) ; or from an act of the understanding when the meaning of some word would grow upon her, or when she realised the beauty and fascination of Him in whose presence she knelt. To Teresa, most certainly, prayer did not consist in ' thinking of nothing ' and making only acts of the will. It consisted, for her part, in finding fuel for the fire, in stirring the soul till of its own accord it bursts into flame ; in realising Jesus Christ her Lord present with her, in dwelling on Him and all He stood for to her, then at last, when He replied to her longing and said ' Come ! ' in leaping out on the rolling waters to reach Him. Sometimes, especially after she had long passed her fiftieth year, there was no need of such preparation. The ' presence ' had become habitual, and she saw and loved at the first moment of recollection. But even then she knew what years of toil it had cost her, and she never ceased to warn her subjects against seeking it before God's own time.

Hence, when we speak of the use of ' memory, understanding, and will,' and treat them as different ' points ' in meditation, thereby making prayer ' discursive ' in the most material sense, we do not rightly express the ' method ' of St. Ignatius, or of St. Teresa, for in this explicitly they are the same. Memory, understanding, and will are not different ' points,' to be traced one after the other ; they go together to make up the same point, as he expressly explains. They are the saint's way of applying to prayer the commandment : ' Thou shalt love the Lord thy God with thy whole heart and thy whole soul, with thy whole mind and thy whole strength.' To love with the whole soul is to love with all the faculties of the soul, and not with

one only ; to love with the whole mind demands
the service of the whole understanding. The more
it is filled with the thought, the recollection, the
' memory ' of God, the better it will pray ; the more
it knows Him, understands Him however inade-
quately, the better it will bow down before Him and
pray. It is a platitude of psychology that the will
follows the understanding ; an act of the will which
rests on nothing but subjective feeling may be
prayer, but it is of a far less solid kind and may
even be unsound. Such prayer, though prayer of
memory and understanding, of recollection and
realisation, need not in the least be ' discursive,' in
the sense in which the word is usually employed,
much less must it be ' discursive,' as some would
assert. It is akin to the contemplation of the artist,
who just looks at a work of art and sees in it beauty
and perfection, who looks at it again and sees yet
more, who, the longer he contemplates, the more
he sees and admires. Such contemplation cannot truly be called ' discursive ' ; it is ' seeing '
more and more. With him, and with the man
who truly prays with memory and understanding,
often enough it happens that he comes away from
his contemplation unable to speak a word. He has
seen so much, he has understood so much, that his
tongue is paralysed. He has learnt by experience
that if he would ' discourse ' on the subject of his
meditation or contemplation, or if he would write
about it, he must stop his prayer. He must come
down to earth, ' think the matter out ' in the terms of
human knowledge, feeling all the while that his
prayer-knowledge, while it supplies the material
for the other, is in itself of quite another kind. And

M

when he gives ' points ' of meditation for others he can only speak in human words, and in the manner of human thought ; but his purpose is not to deliver 'a discourse,' it is to supply through the intellect the fuel which will set the soul on fire, after which memory and understanding may be left to themselves. The giver of ' points ' must try to stir the heart through the brain ; if he merely stirs the understanding he considers he has failed.

Hence when we study the use of the words ' memory, understanding, and will,' as used by St. Ignatius, it must be remembered that he speaks, not as one who is himself praying, but as one who would help another to pray. Though he keeps the three words apart, and repeats them separately, still it is important to notice how in practice, when he develops his point, he joins them together. Thus taking the first point of the first meditation, which is his first use of the words, he says :

> ' The first point will be to take the memory over the first sin, and then the understanding over the same, reasoning, and then the will, wishing to remember and understand all this in order to shame and confound myself the more.'

Memory of the sin, understanding of the sin, wishing, by memory and understanding, to confound myself the more—that is the whole point. The two first are the foundation of the third, but the third is the whole substance of the point ; we remember, we realise, solely that, in the remembrance and realisation, we may have compunction. How else can true compunction be secured ?  The saint then illustrates his meaning, using this first sin as an example :

> ' I say, to call to mind [i.e. to use the memory over] the sin of the angels [thus] : how they were created in grace, how they were unwilling to assist themselves, etc., how they came to pride, how they were changed from grace to malice, how they were cast down from heaven to hell.'

This, be it noticed, is called the use of the memory only, though many, in describing what they would call the Ignatian method, speak of it as the ' discursive ' use of the understanding. They are not wholly wrong in so doing, for the simple reason that even St. Ignatius, who loved careful distinction in his exposition, cannot keep memory and understanding apart. As the soul recalls it realises ; as it concentrates it realises the more ; memory cannot recall without stirring the whole soul to respond. Hence when the saint comes to describe the work of the understanding he finds he has already said all he had to say :

> ' And thereupon in this way to discover more in detail with the understanding.'

Keep on looking ' in this way,' he tells the exercitant, and you will see more and more what this First Sin meant. You need not force yourself to reason ; just look at the event, and let it tell its own tale, realise it, and let your soul react. But with what purpose ? For the sake of the detail, for the sake of understanding better ? That would not be prayer ; it would be study, or at best

emotion. It is prayer only when the whole soul
has been moved, when will has followed memory
and understanding. His answer is :

> ' All this [mark the all-inclusiveness of his pur-
> pose] in order to shame and confound myself
> the more, bringing into comparison with a single
> sin of the angels my so many sins ; and whereas
> they for one sin went to hell, how many times I
> have deserved it for so many.'

Then he adds :

> ' Thereupon to move the affections more by
> the will.'

In the first of these quotations we may notice
how, just as before when speaking of the memory,
so now when speaking of the will, the saint is
unable to describe either the one or the other
adequately without bringing in the understanding.
So is it, and so must it be, with every human attempt
to describe the inner heart of prayer ; since we
must use words we must express what we have to
say in that which appeals to the intellect. But this
by no means implies that the prayer itself is what
is called ' discursive.' It understands more though
it does not reason, it sees more without argument,
the very certainty of its knowledge shows that it
has not been gained by the dubious process of
premiss and conclusion. Hence, if we attempt to
express in concrete form the process of thought in
the first point, it is important to remember that
each step is a further ' seeing,' not a further conclusion ; it is the result of clearer understanding,
not of discursive reasoning as such. With that

postulate, the dealings of the soul with God, still more of God with the soul, in the first point of the first Exercise may be described somewhat as follows, the writer being compelled to use words where the thought in the heart of the one who prays may possibly have need for no words at all :

My God and my Lord, present all about me, present within me, knowing me through and through, so that nothing at all can be hidden from your sight, knowing me far better than I know myself, and yet for all that pitying me, loving me, longing for me ;

Help me that here and now, in this hour of prayer which I wish to be spent really in earnest, my mind, my heart, my body, all myself, may be occupied wholly with you and for you, for your service, for your praise, O Lord of all, Majesty Divine.

[It is important that this preliminary attitude, which St. Ignatius insists upon before every Exercise, meditation or contemplation, during the whole retreat, directs the exercitant and his own perfection, but wholly to God.  Each meditation is primarily, not a step in his own perfection, but an act of service and praise of God.  It is the first lesson of the Foundation, steadily kept in mind ; God's praise, reverence, and service first, and after that the salvation of the man's soul.]

I am here before you, this creature which is my isolated self, a prisoner in ' the body of this death,' an exile in ' the valley of this darkness,' a companion with the animals of this earth ;  I, with a soul that is made for so much more than they, for the true life, for you.

I would it were different, I 'want and desire,'
long with all my heart, that it should be different.

I would be ashamed for anything that has
brought me to this, that has made me no better
than the beasts.

I would be filled with confusion, for that is only
truth, at what I am, at what I have made myself,
at the sins I have committed, the offences against
you, the degradation of myself,

Seeing how many sin has ruined,
Seeing how often I have deserved the same,
The same for ever.
I look at this thing sin
I see it in its first beginning
One sin brought down the angels
The angels created in grace
Making them unwilling to pay reverence to their
Creator and Lord
Unwilling to obey Him
Unwilling to use their freedom aright
Using it only for themselves
Making themselves their own masters
Making themselves the Lord
Defying their Creator
Coming to pride
Accepting it and its consequences
Created in noble grace, transformed into hideous
malice
Created in beautiful love, transformed into cruel
hatred
And that is the story of sin everywhere
In peoples and nations
In individuals, in myself
Sin destroys the beauty of God's creature

Sin destroys the life of grace
Sin destroys freedom
Sin destroys right order
Sin destroys love
Sin creates malice
Sin fosters hatred
Sin turns heaven into hell
What then must sin be !
What must sin of mine be !
If others knew me as sin has made me, how I
would be ashamed !
If they knew even what I know, how I would be
confounded !
Yet He knows far better than I know.
What have I done ?
What am I doing ?
What shall I do ?

                    Our Father.


In some such exposition as this it may be shown
how every point in every meditation of the Exercises is not an argument, a process of ' discursive
reasoning,' but a prayer, a vision, gaining in
insight as the time proceeds.   Memory, understanding, and will are blended into one ;  they are
no more than the natural and necessary instruments
for every prayer that comes from the soul itself,
and every other prayer, as St. Teresa repeatedly
says, must be left to Him who gives it.

The other two ' points ' of this first meditation
may be easily and naturally drawn out in exactly
the same way as the first.   Each adds something
more to the realisation of sin, each gives further
insight, more understanding, adds more to shame

and confusion, and to the shunning of the source of all evil. We may therefore pass them over in the present study and come to what St. Ignatius calls the Colloquy.

It is urged against him and his ' method ' that he relegates the colloquy to the end of his meditation, whereas the true soul of prayer will be engaged in colloquy of some kind all the time. Here again we have to remember that the saint is setting out the points and matter for meditation, he is not making or describing the meditation itself. He sets everything in order, memory, understanding, will, colloquy ; nevertheless in actual practice he knows that they cannot be so separated. He places the Colloquy at the end ; nevertheless, as he has shown clearly enough in the Annotations, ' the end ' may come anywhere at all, and at any time, in the course of the meditation. As soon as a soul has attained what it seeks, he tells us again and again, then let it rest contented, and not attempt to proceed any further. In other words, there let it overflow in becoming affections and colloquies, in whatever way it may please, expressing the grief of its heart, or whatever else overflows within it. This only he would insist upon, and in this he is at one with all the saints of prayer before him and after him, that prayer is not truly prayer without affection and colloquy of some kind.

Since the saint has made so much of ' colloquy ' it is reasonable to expect that in describing it he should reveal something of his own mind and heart. We are not mistaken ; for here, perhaps more than anywhere else, we recognise the man of prayer. For colloquy, to him, is very intimate indeed ; it is, from the very first, 'just as one friend speaks to another, or a servant to his master.' It is intimate, with that intimacy which makes equal, which is not afraid to be seen through and through, which will be utterly trusting in spite of its confusion and shame, which will ask in need of Him whom it blindly trusts, and therefore already loves, whether for forgiveness, or for a favour, or for counsel. Thus he describes the movement of the soul :

'Now asking for some favour, now blaming himself for some ill deed, now disclosing his affairs and seeking counsel in them.'

It is very real, very familiar, God is in the room with the exercitant and they are holding converse together. To a soul which prays in that way the supernatural has already become all-absorbing ; and yet we are still engaged with the first Exercise of the Retreat !

In this spirit, then, as it were securing that prayer shall dominate all the rest, the meditation or contemplation is described as ending with the colloquy. It is not that memory, understanding, and will are shut off ; they are used just as much as before, and for the same reason, that the colloquy itself cannot be described without them. But now there is a difference of orientation. In the points, as was announced in the third prelude, the soul was taught to look on sin, and to see in it cause for its own shame and confusion ; in the colloquy we are made to dwell on the still greater, and utterly undeserved, shame and confusion sin has brought on Jesus Christ Our Lord. First the shame of

angels, then the shame of men, then the shame of a
soul condemned, each time ending with shame of
our own ; but now the shame and confusion of
Jesus Our Lover, made so real that we see the
bleeding body, so real that we forget our own
shame in our longing to relieve that of another.
In other words, in the colloquy we pass already
from attrition to contrition ; for shame and sorrow
for our own sake, however humiliating, is only
attrition ; shame, sorrow, resolution, for the sake
of Christ is the sorrow that is truly contrite. Jesus
Christ Our Lord is present ; Friend in need and
in deed, Master, Servant, letting me call Him
whatever I will. He is placed upon the cross before
my eyes ; He, my Creator, now become Man for
love of me ; He, possessor of eternal life, meeting
temporal death for me ; He the all-innocent, bearing the shame and confusion of my sins for me.
Let me look at Him, ' such as He is,' the actual
fact of Calvary ; St. Ignatius is not content that
our prayer should be a feat of the imagination
only, he wants me to see the Crucified ' such as
He is.' Let me be there, seeing Him hanging on
the cross. Let me realise why He is there ;
through me, and in me, and for me. Let my
heart speak, as it may be prompted. Let me, to
use the saint's own words, ' discourse of what may
offer itself.' This is what I have done for Christ,
and what He has done for me. What am I now
doing for Him ? After this what shall I do ?

The saint has just made use of the word ' discourse.' But it is in a very different sense from
that implied in the usual use of the phrase ' discursive prayer.' The latter implies ' reasoning ' in

the heart of the meditation ; the former comes
into action only when ' meditation ' is almost over,
and the soul gropes about for the means to satisfy
its contrition and love. ' Reasoning ' leaves us
where we were ; ' discoursing ' in colloquy is the
gateway to contemplation of the very highest kind,
such indeed as is enjoyed and described by the most
sublime contemplatives. Yet we are still only at
the First Exercise. Such is its goal, to be reached
as soon as possible ; when it is reached all the rest
may be set aside, even the points of the Exercise.
The beginner, or the soul not much given to
prayer, may not at first realise the full significance
of the colloquy. It will, at first, be naturally occupied with itself, with its own misdeeds, its own
shame and confusion. Indeed there will be some,
perhaps many, who will be able to go no further ;
for these St. Ignatius has already expressly said
that it will be enough to stop at this point. But
there are others who will see more, and it is these
whom the saint has in mind. In time, it may be
by dint of repetition, the reality of Jesus crucified
grows upon them. They come to see Him, in
' imagination ' it may be, but none the less knowing
that what they see is true. The fascination of that
living presence grows, takes the soul out of itself ;
with Christ it is nailed to the cross, and henceforth
it carries the wounds of Christ on itself, it longs to
make up what is wanting in the sufferings of Christ.
All this is contained in the very First Exercise, and,
as we shall presently see, St. Ignatius would have
it repeated and repeated until it has sunk per-
manently down into the soul, never to be effaced ;
until, that is, love of Jesus crucified has involved its

own crucifixion. The meditation began with a petition for its own shame and confusion ; it has ended with the discovery of the shame and confusion of Christ. Its own shame has been swallowed up in His shame ; now His shame makes it long to be shamed. Before, its shame was accepted as the due reward of its sin ; now its sorrow is turned into joy that it may share in His shame, because He has shared with ours.

# VII

## THE SECOND EXERCISE

IT is not unimportant to notice that this Second
Exercise follows immediately on the First, that
is, in the same morning, after a sufficient inter-
val of rest.  It should not be deferred to another
day ; in the repetitions which follow the two are to
be taken as one.  The reason is that it is part of
the First, its application to the exercitant himself ;
and therefore the sooner it is made after the meaning of the First has been grasped the deeper will
be its effect.  The First Exercise has dwelt rather
on Sin in itself, and on the Sinner in general ; even
when it has come to application it has not descended
to detail.  As with Nathan and David, as with
Jesus and the Pharisees, St. Ignatius will first have
us realise the enormity of Sin under conditions in
which we are not likely to be biased ; only when
our indignation has been roused, and we ourselves
have demanded atonement, does the Prophet really
turn on us and say : ' Thou art the man ! '  In
this way the two Exercises are one.  The exercitant
has broken his prayer that he may give body and
soul a rest ; he comes back to it, ready once more
to love ' with his whole heart and his whole soul,
with his whole mind and his whole strength,' and
continues where he left off.  He recalls again the
presence in which he prays ; he sees himself as he

saw himself before, indeed more clearly now than before, body and soul, corruptible and corrupted, exiled in the valley of this death, the companion, by desert at least, of the brute, instinct-dominated beasts. It is no exaggeration, it is the plain truth, to his shame and confusion, and he is oppressed beneath the burthen. To have a sense of this oppression at this moment is true prayer ; it is the beginning of humility, and contrition, and fear of the Lord, and therefore the beginning of wisdom, that is, of greater understanding of the mind and heart of God. Soon he shall be relieved of it ; but first, that the discarding may be the more complete, let him realise what it is that has so disfigured him, and what have been its effects. He has seen what were those effects in the angels, in man, in a lost soul, in Jesus crucified ; let him now see what it is, what are its effects, actually, in matter of fact, without any exaggeration, in himself.

But this Second Exercise is very much more than an examination of conscience, or a preparation for a General Confession. As with all the Exercises, its purpose is contained in the Prelude of Petition ; and this cannot be read, knowing that the author was not given to exaggeration, without our being struck by the height of prayer which it assumes to have been already reached.

> ' The second [prelude] is to ask for what I want. Here it will be to beg for ever-growing and intense sorrow, and tears, for my sins.'

Before, it had been only ' shame and confusion,' one might say a special state of soul, induced chiefly by consideration of sin and its effects in other victims. Now it is 'sorrow and tears,' two very different things, induced by consideration of my own sins and their effects in myself. Before 'shame and confusion' had been a torture, at the end made welcome because of their union with the 'shame and confusion' of Christ crucified ; now they are almost welcomed for their own sake, as a means of atonement for my own misdeeds. Sorrow is repenting for something wrongly done ; it is wishing that it had never happened ; it is a longing to put right the evil and injury ; it is determining that the like shall never happen again ; and it is all this from the motives of love. Sorrow springs from love or it is not sorrow ; it is merely remorse, or disillusion, or self-blame, which, in the things that matter, bear no fruit. But sorrow that is born of love has in it the immortality of love and can never die ; on the contrary, the more with time the soul's eyes are opened, and it sees what its sins have done, so much the more will it grow in intensity and in its effects. Abiding sorrow for sin is characteristic of the saints, perhaps especially of the great contemplatives. That is to say, the greatest saints are the greatest sorrowers ; there never comes a time when they can set their sins aside, when they can say they need not sorrow any more. *Peccatum meum contra me est semper.*

[It is precisely in this that the Catholic tradition differs from a certain tendency in modern spirituality. The true man of prayer, the holier he becomes, that is, the more closely he is drawn by the love of God, so much the more does he realise his own unworthiness, and sorrows for his sins, till at last because of them he cannot restrain his tears.

To him the ' gift of tears ' is not only one of the ' consolations ' of prayer ; very often, perhaps always, he can scarcely say whether he weeps for sorrow or for joy. His joy is founded on sorrow, his sorrow is turned into joy, and the two are never very far apart. Hence when St. Ignatius speaks of ' tears for my sins ' he is not using hyperbole, he is not speaking in metaphor. He means exactly what he says, that if the exercitant cannot yet burst into ' tears because of his sins,' he should pray that one day he may ; and one day the soul whose sorrow is ' ever-growing ' in intensity will find, almost in spite of itself, how true is his meaning. Yet what is this but a call to sublime experiences in prayer ? And that already in only the second exercise of the series.]

We are endeavouring to show in this study how keenly St. Ignatius strove in his Exercises to make above all things else a man of prayer ; and that, not merely a prayerful man, but a man who, if God so favoured him, might rise to the highest experiences of contemplation. This, we would maintain, was his first purpose ; if he could make such a man, he knew that all the rest would follow, without this there would be little hope of rising above a human standard. Nevertheless he knew there was one great danger ; in making such a man, especially at the beginning, there was danger of unreality, of false horizons, of insufficient consideration of the actual facts of life. This must be secured ; and the first point in this Second Exercise is perhaps the most conspicuous instance, at least it is the first, of the saint's unbending realism ; of his determination not to be side-tracked, not even by his own ideal, not by any kind of prayer whatsoever, from looking at the truth and standing by it. We can be ashamed, confounded, sorrowful, affected unto tears, moved by the sight of the sufferings of Christ, in other ways lifted up in prayer, and yet it may be only emotion ; all such experiences may be soothing to the soul, they may give the impression of deep prayer, and yet in practice they may lead nowhere. Such prayer, as experience had taught him, was far removed from that deeply-rooted prayer of the saints which, however sublime, is never separated from the actualities of the soul itself. The former would leave this life alone, and would rise to heaven at once without its body ; the latter cannot forget that such an ambition and assumption is essentially unreal, that the soul in this life is the form of the body, and that it is what it is in the sight of God and nothing more, responsible for the body as for itself. St. Ignatius knew, as had been the teaching of the saints from St. Peter and St. Paul, that the first condition of all true prayer is sinlessness ; and first condition of sinlessness is a clear knowledge of one's own misdeeds : 'Blessed are the clean of heart, for they shall see God.' Other beginnings of prayer were taught by some in his time, but he knew they were cheap and produced only imita-tions ; if a man can only be allowed to ignore his liabilities, his responsibilities, his misdeeds, to become a saint would be a comparatively easy matter. But he knew otherwise ; he knew that to become a saint was the hardest thing in the world, and that the way of prayer was anything but the fascinating thing that some proposed. It

N

was a hard way, all the harder because the most sublime.

Hence, after the first introduction, he now begins to teach the way of prayer in earnest : *initium sapientiae timor Domini.* Let the soul begin by learning itself, its own evil deeds and the truth of itself that they reveal. Let it not be troubled, for the present, that this study of itself may seem to be taking it away from the knowledge of God and His Christ ; before one builds one must dig into the ground for foundations. It will find, even in this Exercise, to say nothing of what may come after, that the more, and the deeper, and the more sincerely it dwells on this single point, so much the more quickly will God come to it, and that is the secret of all sublime prayer.

The second point goes deeper still. The mere sight of the number of times, now gathered into one great whole, that one has been a delinquent in the service of God is bad enough, but the very number may dull the soul's recognition of the significance of each act, and of their cumulative effect. Apart from the ruin sin brings, on the angelic nature, on the human race, on every soul that has offended, even on the human Christ Himself, there is the consideration of the very act of sin. Sin in itself, leaving aside its effects, is a loathsome thing ; it is the act of a coward and worse, it is a manifestation of the worst side of human nature, which is malice. The doing of sin because it is evil, destroying for the sake of destruction, brings man down, not only, as was seen before, to the level of the beast, but to the level of the devils in hell. We see foul deeds done, and we say that such

deeds are 'inhuman,' that men of themselves, in
their sober, reasonable moments, could never do
such things. Yet St. Ignatius would have us consider how we ourselves, though, perhaps, in a less
dramatic way, have done the like, have at least
acted in such a way that, weighed in the balance,
we would be found on the side of bestiality, of
inhumanity, of reckless destruction of all that is
best in human nature. He would have us consider

'the foulness, the malice, which every mortal sin
contains in itself, even if it were not forbidden.'

'Even if it were not forbidden.' There are
some unbelievers who maintain that nothing is
forbidden, that everything is permitted, and therefore that there is no such thing as sin ; since they
recognise no God, they cannot recognise moral
evil. But even these, unless they have become
depraved beyond hope of human appeal, will not
say that to dishonour one's parents, to mutilate a
fellow-man, to shame a good woman, to steal, to
lie, are anything but foul, degrading, malicious,
bringing man below the beast, that does not naturally do any of these things. Such philosophers,
frankly, may take the life of the beast as their
standard ; by doing so they lower the life of man
beneath it, for even they will allow that what we
call sin, 'even if not forbidden,' lowers a man
below the behaviour of the beast : St. Ignatius, in
this point, would have me see how much and how
often I have degraded myself, judged only by that
standard. 'I am not worthy that I should enter
into thy sight; I am not worthy that Thou shouldst
enter under my roof.' And yet the more sincerely

and fervently I can say that prayer, acknowledging the facts without any effort to hide them, to explain them away, to justify them by some philosophical subterfuge, the more certain it is that the Lord will hear and come.

The first two points have considered my sins and their foulness, the rest consider the sinner himself. It begins from the opposite end. It is a meditation for humility, the finding of the truth, and therefore the right estimate, about oneself. Human nature, such is its perversity, is prone to think cruel things about others, it resents these same things when applied to itself. Once more, as so often, St. Ignatius, who ' knew what was in man,' has taken his cue from human nature. The exercitant may resent the belittling of himself in his own eyes ; St. Ignatius only asks him, not to do as he would be done by, but to do to himself what he often finds himself doing to others, especially to those whom he dislikes or envies. Does he not resent their elevation above their equals ? And yet, whatever he may wish to think about himself, is he not, in matter of fact, a very small thing indeed in comparison with the rest of mankind ? This is true, no matter how good, and innocent, and even personally gifted he may be ; but when he considers himself in detail, in soul and in body, it is only by refusing to measure himself against his fellow men that he can hold up his head at all. Nay more, he knows that many do not like him, belittle him, make nothing of him, and much as he resents it he knows that their judgement is not without reason. Whatever to some he may appear, however they may esteem him, he is well aware that those who ignore him are in most ways nearer the truth. And this, considering him merely as he is, just the human being ; but if they knew all, if they knew his inner sinfulness, the harm he has done and the harm he is capable of doing, the injury to others ; if they could with their senses realise what in fact he has made himself, if he could see himself as the angels see him, as possibly some saint of God sees him who chances to pass him by, then he would

'look upon himself as a wound and ulcer [in the body of mankind], whence have come forth so many sins and so many iniquities, and poison so utterly foul.'

But the truth of this will be realised only by the man of prayer and through prayer. Without prayer language such as this, and a concept such as this, will either be ignored or it will be declared to be exaggerated, fantastic, or merely morbid. The man who does not pray never gets free from himself ; he lives, however little he may reflect upon it, in an artificial world of his own creation, self-deceived. Such a man is as great in his own esteem as he fancies himself to be, let other men be what they may ; he is, to himself, anything but 'a wound and ulcer' on the body of mankind, no matter what harm he may be doing to others by his self-esteem, his self-seeking, his example, his influence, his satisfaction of himself at their expense, and the like. He seeks his own satisfaction ; what happens to others is their affair. But the man of prayer sees further than himself ; he learns to see himself, and all life, independently of himself; and when he has seen himself in that perspective and proportion he is not slow to discover his own littleness and unimportance, and the meanness of the deeds which, looking to himself alone, he had made of no account or had even thought matter for boasting. Such a discovery of one's real self is the true foundation of prayer, and to abide in it always is a guarantee of true progress.

The soul that has thus discovered itself is then in a fit condition to make the next step : *Domine Jesu, noverim me, noverim te.* It may now look up to God and learn to know Him ; and it can begin to know Him best, most surely and with greater ultimate result, by learning what its faith teaches it about Him. Here is the beginning of that path which may lead in time to the sublimest contemplation ; already the saint gives the soul a first hint of that vision which was the source of his own ecstasies and raptures. It is true we cannot know God as He is ; the theologians tell us that we know about Him what He is not. Nevertheless prayer cannot be addressed to a mere negative ; the soul cannot love that which is not ; though we know God only by analogy, yet, as far as it goes, our knowledge must be true that we may praise, reverence, and serve Him. St. Ignatius, at this point, introduces the soul to God by way of this analogy. He speaks of His attributes, the only safe way by which we are able, with our limited understanding, to learn what He is ; in particular He chooses four, because of the ease with which the contrast with the human creature can be made.

The Lord God, the infinite wisdom, who knows

and rules all things, from whom nothing is concealed, who guides all things to their perfect end : myself, whose wisdom mainly consists in knowing my own unwisdom and stupidity ; the more wise I become, the more I discover my own folly, indeed it is my folly that chiefly makes me wise.

The Lord God, the infinite power and strength, the omnipotent who ruleth from end to end mightily and disposeth all things sweetly ; myself, only too conscious of my inability to do anything at all worth while ; the more I have done, the more I have discovered that I have not done, the more I can do, the more I discover I cannot do : *velle quidem mihi adjacet, perficere autem non invenio.* On the contrary, the evil I would not, that I do ; often enough my one hope of forgiveness lies in the cry that I seem to be unable to help myself.

The Lord God, the infinitely perfect justice, none the less perfect because it is tempered with infinitely perfect mercy : myself, a creature of prejudice and presumption, so that even my faith can sometimes be presented to me as one of these ; a creature always and wholly biased in my own favour ; a creature that is clever in its own defence, justifying at times its iniquity, of which it is only too conscious. And this, it would almost seem, from its very nature ; human nature seems so unable to be true and just that many in despair ask, What is truth ? What is justice ?

The Lord God, infinite goodness—we cannot even begin to imagine what this means, and yet we know that it is and must be true. Not only is He all good, not only does He contain pre-eminently in Himself everything that is beautiful, admirable, lovable, but He is that which they stand for, He is that which makes them what they are, the substance of which they are the shadow. He is them all, they are what they are only because He is; without Him as their source, without Him whom in being they reflect, without Him as their purpose and goal, they would lose their beauty and goodness. He is the all good, He is essential goodness.

[The student of the Exercises will notice how here already the final 'Contemplation to obtain Love' is being foreshadowed. Here in the midst of the 'meditation or contemplation' on my own unlovable self, the vision of the love of God is made to appear.]

In contrast with this, myself—What is there in me that is good? This only, that like other creatures I am a reflex of God; for the rest, what is there that is beautiful or lovable, how much that is the opposite!

This assuredly is not 'discursive' meditation in the ordinary sense in which the word is used. It is not 'reasoning' as the term is understood, though it may be 'reasoning' in the sense of St. Ignatius, St. John of the Cross and St. Teresa. It is true contemplation, 'acquired' it may be, but none the less contemplation, in a recognised meaning of the word. It is 'looking on this picture and on that,' and seeing the contrast; and the more one sees, contemplates, realises without 'discoursing,' the more will the vision have its effect. For this very reason the saint has warned the giver of the Exercises against over-elaboration. Let him not give the exercitant too much 'to think about,' let him give him much to see, and let him open his eyes that he may see it, and then let him leave him with God.   Hence, when he comes to the fifth point, St. Ignatius no longer speaks even in the language of ' discourse ' ;  he does no more than attempt to describe the soul as the truth with its consequences grows upon it :

> ' The fifth :  an exclamation of wonder with ever-growing emotion, passing in review all creatures, how they have left me in life and preserved me in it :  the angels, though they are the sword of divine justice, how they have borne with me and protected and prayed for me : the saints, how they have been interceding and praying for me ;  and the heavens, sun, moon, stars, and elements, fruits, birds, fish, and animals ;  and the earth, how it has not opened itself to swallow me up, creating new hells that I might suffer for ever in them.'

This is the description of a vision, it is not an argument ;  it partakes more of Æschylus than of Aristotle, of Plato the visionary than of Plato the dialectician.   It sees all creation, and itself in the midst, with the all-loving God above, offended yet holding His hand, restraining creation that would ' call down fire from heaven ' on the guilty offender. The whole of this point is little more than a summary of many pages in St. Bonaventure's *Stimulus Divini Amoris*.   The ' sorrow and tears ' are at last brought to their fullness, not by the vengeance of God but by its restraint ;  not by threat of punishment, but by the realisation of love and mercy, of God and of all His creatures by whose co-operation I live.   It is a vision which, once it has been seen, will be revived in various forms during the Exercises till it reaches its climax in the Contemplation for obtaining Love ; and if the last is truly a source of contemplation, no less is this.

# CONCLUSION

LET us try to sum up the contents of this study. Whatever may be said about the character of St. Ignatius Loyola, his supposed military genius, his driving personality, the work he accomplished, one thing is certain ; none of these, nor all of them together, give us the real key to the man himself. He wrote one book, or the main outline of it, early in his spiritual life ; his other book took him the rest of his years on earth to write. He was, as was said of him by those who knew him best, a man of comparatively few ideas, even of few virtues ; but these went deep, and were then allowed to grow as grace, and experience and learning from other men developed them. The Book of the Spiritual Exercises was and is scarcely a book at all ; it is rather the portrait of a deep conviction, made as brief as possible, with every word weighed, altered, and added to from time to time, and then left in the shape of notes for those to interpret who had tried to apply them. Their inspiration came from many sources ; from different religious, while the author himself was yet a layman, from different books, to one who could not be said to be learned, and therefore studied single books all the more. But whatever the sources, Inigo was one who took nothing ' on faith,' as we call it. He tested each lesson, or inspiration, as it came, and made it his own ; if he found, by experience in himself, that it was profitable, he wrote it down, if he did not he passed it by.  Hence, in spite of the echoes from other works to be found in his Book, it was, nevertheless, entirely his own ; indeed so much his own that the less careful reader may easily imagine it to be unlike others of its kind.

In this Book, then, the true Ignatius Loyola is to be found ; not so much in the work he did, unless that work is also interpreted by means of the Book.  He is known to have said that had the Society of Jesus been suppressed it might have made him sad for ten minutes ; after all, the Society was an afterthought, it grew, like other Orders, from a spirit working amid certain circumstances ; it was never the beginning and end of his ideal.  Nor was obedience the first of the virtues he set before those he drew about him ; though later, again as a result of experience, he wished it to be the firm bond of their union, yet he founded even this on a firmer bond still, and that was the bond of love, the *vinculum caritatis*, the *interna caritatis et amoris lex*, stressed on every page of his Constitutions.  But for this there was needed the true man ; the man who could love to the utmost, to the extent of fullest sacrifice, so that wherever true love led he would go.  For the making of such a man Exercises, a course of training, was needed ; when we come to examine that course we find that, from beginning to end, one thing, and one thing alone, is stressed, and that is growth in prayer.  Prayer will free a man from all impediments ; prayer will show him, as nothing else will show him, in what truth of life consists. Prayer will open his mind to the big things of life ; prayer will give him the means to attain them. Prayer will develop love, as nothing else will develop it. Prayer will turn love into suffering, and suffering into love, making the true man rejoice that he is accounted worthy to suffer, so that suffering is joy.

Such is the material out of which were formed the Spiritual Exercises ; they are, first and foremost, exercises for the making of the true man, and that by means of prayer. It is, in some sense, a dangerous process ; by no other means may a man be more easily deceived ; he will experience joy of soul that he has never known before, distress of soul which may, at times, drive him to the brink of despair ; at least if the man himself is of the stuff Ignatius looks for, the stuff of which heroes are made. Hence such a man needs to be carefully guided, for often enough he will be unable to guide himself. Sometimes the darkness will be too black, sometimes the light will be too blinding, and he will be tempted to be rash. Let him, then, learn from the beginning to be firm ; to live through darkness unchanged, knowing it will have an end, to continue on in prayer though at times it seems to be empty and futile, to live in God, and with God, making every spiritual trial draw him the more to the feet of God. So, too, with the man who experiences the joy of prayer. Let him, too, beware of being rash and imprudent ; let him remember that this joy will not endure for ever ; let him learn from his rejoicing that it is good for him to adhere to the Lord, so that when trial comes he may be firm. Throughout these first beginnings the saint has his eye on one thing, and one thing only. He does not ask for a strong man, he asks for one with ' large heart and liberality towards his Creator and Lord.' He troubles little about resolutions ; what he seeks is ' the clean of heart ' that he may see God, and it is the discovery of God that he makes his one criterion.

*The Mayflower Press, Plymouth.*  William Brendon & Son, Ltd.